AMC
MUSCLE CARS

LARRY G. MITCHELL

MBI Publishing
Company

First published in 2000 by MBI Publishing Company, 729 Prospect Avenue, PO Box 1, Osceola, WI 54020-0001 USA

MBI Publishing Company books are also available at discounts in bulk quantity for industrial or sales-promotional use. For details write to Special Sales Manager at Motorbooks International Wholesalers & Distributors, 729 Prospect Avenue, PO Box 1, Osceola, WI 54020-0001 USA.

Library of Congress Cataloging-in-Publication Data
    Mitchell, Larry G.
       AMC muscle cars / Larry G. Mitchell
         p. cm. — (Musclecar color history)
       Includes index.
       ISBN 0-7603-0761-X (alk. paper)
       1. American Motors automobiles—History
       2. Muscle cars—History I. Title. II. Musclecar
       color history
    TL215.A44 M5797 2000

Printed in Hong Kong

On the front cover: *The Big Bad Green 1969 1/2 AMX 500 Special and the Plum Metallic 1974 Javelin AMX led AMC's high-performance charge during the musclecar wars. The AMX was the only American two-seat high-performance sports car besides the Corvette. Fitted with a 315-horsepower 390 V-8, the AMX was more than a match for many of Detroit's finest high-performance cars. The low-slung, hump-fendered Javelin was built from 1971 to 1974. Equipped with a 401 V-8, it generated about 270 horsepower. Doug Eiriksen of Colorado Springs, Colorado, owns the AMX 500, and the Javelin AMX belongs to John Thompson of Denver, Colorado. Jerry Heasley*

On the frontispiece: *The 1969 1/2 SC/Rambler 390 V-8 rode on attractive blue-painted rally wheels, that were part of the bad-to-the-bone paint scheme. Larry G. Mitchell*

On the title page: *The timeless styling, nimble handling, and large displacement engines gave this musclecar a character all of its own. With a 390 V-8 under the hood, the 97-inch wheel base AMX could turn quarter-mile times in the 14-second range and get to 60 miles per hour from a standing stop in the high-6s. Larry Mitchell collection*

On the back cover: Top: *The mighty 1969-1/2 Rambler Hurst SC/Rambler "A" Model's bold and brash hood scoop and graphics set it apart from the crowd. A 390 V-8 produced 315-horsepower, and a 4-speed Hurst manual transmission carried power to the rear wheels. This is one rare car—only 1,512 SC/Ramblers were built. Bruce Jacobsen* **Bottom:** *The 1970 Rebel Machine was easily identified with its Frost White paint accompanied by red, white, and blue reflective decals. The 340-horsepower 390 V-8 featured a higher lift cam as well as special intake and exhaust manifolds. This provided better breathing to create a boost in horsepower. Larry Mitchell*

Designed by Arthur Durkee

Contents

Acknowledgments

A special "thank you" goes out to the members of the Classic AMX Club International (CACI) and American Motorsport International (AMSI) who allowed their cars to be photographed for this book. These two American Motors collector clubs make up AMC World Clubs, Inc., and were founded by myself.

I'd like to thank the photographers who helped out such as my special friend and professional automotive photographer, Jerry Heasley, who flew up from his home in Pampa, Texas, when I needed help to shoot the cover. Jerry also shot or supplied some additional photographs used in this book.

There were additional photographers who contributed their work to this book. The first is my long-time friend, Bruce W. Jacobsen. Bruce and I first met in the summer of 1969 when he drove his new 1969 AMX into the parking lot of the Belvidere, Illinois, Chrysler Assembly Plant as I was getting out of my 1966 1/2 Rogue. We both worked at the plant and discovered we both had a love for AMC cars. Bruce is a charter member of the First National AMC Car Club that he helped found with me over a quarter-of-a-century ago. He and I are the only two original members who have attended all 26 national conventions without missing one—so far. My other club members or friends who also used their cameras to photograph their cars or others' cars for the book are: Adam Ortiz, Mark and Mike Knapp, Dan Behymer, Jeff and Lori Sorenson, Carson (Tony) Zamisch, and David McHattie.

Thanks to those who contributed photos: Mark Ripley, Tom Benvie, Cliff Hohnstein, and Richard A. Teague. Thanks to a man who contributed both historic racing photos and his experiences as a pioneer AMC builder and driver of his own 1967 Super-American in SCCA racing, as well as being Crew Chief and driver for Kaplan Engineering in the Trans-Am Series—John Martin.

My thanks to those club members/AMC car owners who put up with fussy photographers who demanded more time and effort to get a couple of shots than they as car owners ever expected: Jim Zelenski, Werner Fruhwirth, Russell Sizemore, Richard Owens, Harold Lundy, Jeff and Lori Sorenson, John Thompson, Gary Carlson, John DiCino, Dan Bruerton, Jim Weyand, Wayne Davis, Steve Lawson, Doug Eiriksen, Gene Jones, Roger Scott, Jr. and daughter Amy Scott, Jim Kaufman, Don and Chris Dimm, Bill Smith, Bob Ripley, and Keith Hankel.

All of the slides used for this book were developed by the best lab in Denver, Colorado, Pro Lab. Thanks go out to customer service manager Ron and his staff. Most of the slide film used was Fuji Provia Professional F. I shot nearly 75 percent of the fresh photographs in this book with my new Nikon N90S with a 24mm to 120mm Nikor lens.

This book is dedicated to all the people in the worldwide AMC hobby who have been my club members and friends. It is also dedicated to those who have stood by me and supported me in the good and bad times during my 30 years of working in the AMC hobby. There are a few of you who are the best friends a man could ever hope for. You know who you are, and I thank you from the heart. In the end, life is all about relationships and close friends. The cars are really secondary and incidental.

Since I also dedicated my first book to my father, Floyd Mitchell, I wish to also dedicate this one to my mother, Ann. She put up with me as a toddler, running through her lovely flower bed in the summer of 1947. After a scolding, she made my favorite dinner, tomato soup with a melted slice of American cheese, followed by her banana creme pie. Thanks Mom.

I give a special thanks to my good friend, Werner Fruhwirth, who helped me with the first book I did for MBI Publishing (*AMC Buyer's Guide*), and now this one. He reviewed the manuscript for historical accuracy and reminded me I don't know it all. Werner helped in choosing photos for the layout and in finding needed items from my personal historical collection. Werner deserves some of the credit for this book.

My wife Linda has put up with all this car stuff for over 25 years. She deserves some credit; not all non-car women would have had the patience. Linda was a grade school teacher and spent the time to proofread the manuscript for spelling and grammar. For her efforts, she gets to commandeer the new 2000 Jeep Wrangler we bought and were going to share. I now only have visitation rights to "Y2KTJ" on the weekends.

Any author of history needs to consult the writings of others who have come before. For reference, I used the 3rd Edition of the *Standard Catalog of American Cars*, John Gunnell, editor, published by Krause Publications. *The Unfair Advantage*, by Mark Donohue with Paul Van Valkenburgh, published by Dodd, Mead and Company. *Trans-Am Racing, 1966-85* by Albert R. Bochroch, published by MBI Publishing. *American Motors The Last Independent* by Patrick R. Foster, published by Krause Publications. *Amazing AMC Muscle* by Edrie J. Marquez, published by MBI Publishing. *Mister Javelin, Guy Hadsall, Jr. at American Motors* by Guy Hadsall, Jr., with Sam Fiorani and Patrick R. Foster, published by The Society of Automotive Historians, Inc. Archive information and photos came from the AMC Artifact and Historical Collection in Arvada, Colorado. This is the personal 30-year collection of Larry G. Mitchell.

one

In The Beginning....
AMC's Performance Roots

B efore American Motors became American Motors in 1954, the original company made automobiles under the Nash name starting in 1917. But the company actually dated back to 1902 when a bicycle maker started to make passenger cars in Kenosha, Wisconsin. Thomas B. Jeffery founded the company, and he built the largest automobile plant in the United States at that time, in that little prairie town on the shores of Lake Michigan north of Chicago. The car he built was called the "Rambler," and the name is still known today.

Charlie Nash worked for General Motors but left and bought Jeffery out in 1916. Nash cars were very fine cars indeed, and from the first car that wore Charlie Nash's name in 1917 to the last car in 1957, hundreds of thousands of Nash cars were sold to the American buying public. However, none could be considered serious performance cars. There was one small exception. On February 16, 1951, Nash Motors introduced to the U.S. market a true two-seat sports car called the Nash-Healey. The car was styled by Pininfarina of Italy and was produced from aluminum in Warwick, England, by an agreement with noted race car driver Donald Healey. Nash-Healeys were then imported to America and sold through Nash dealers. These cars were certainly sports cars of their time with traditional open cockpits, seating for only two, and a version of the Nash 252.6-ci six-cylinder with dual carburetors (in the second version of the car). The motor was called the "Le Mans" six. It used overhead valves and produced 140 brake horsepower.

This engine was used in a racing version of the Nash-Healey and was called the Nash Ambassador Le Mans Dual-Jetfire six. The racing Nash-Healey won first place in its class and a third place overall in the 1952 French Grand Prix at Le Mans. It was Nash's first effort to build a serious performance

The Nash-Healey was made from 1951 to 1954 as a two-seat sports car and could be considered the granddaddy of the 1968–1970 AMX. Larry Mitchell collection

9

The 1957 Rambler Rebel was the first true American musclecar, seven years before the 1964 GTO. The recipe was a 255-horsepower 327-ci AMC V-8 in a compact car body. Larry Mitchell

car. Although the 1951–1954 Nash-Healey cars were sold only in handfuls and were designed and manufactured outside the United States, they must be considered the grandfather of the sporty high-performance AMC cars to come in the 1960s, especially the 1968, 1969, and 1970 two-seat AMX.

Nash merged with automotive great, Hudson, in the spring of 1954, and a new company called American Motors Corporation was formed. Hudson had more racing credentials than Nash, especially in circle track racing with noted drivers such as Marshall Teague. But the true Hudson cars ended with the 1954 model run, and the once proud name carried over on thinly disguised Nashes, Ramblers, and Metropolitans for 1955, 1956, and 1957. In 1958 the Hudson name was gone, ending a legend that started in 1910. Nash cars of the 1950s were sold on the basis of interior

comfort, a cushy ride, and gas economy. The famed Nash 600 model was introduced in 1941 and was said to get 30 miles per gallon. With a 20-gallon gas tank, it got 600 miles on one tank of fuel. Sure, conditions were different, but that kind of gas economy was commonplace under the driving conditions of the time.

In 1950, Nash became the prince in the kingdom of fuel economy with the introduction of the "little" 1950 Nash Rambler. The Rambler was one of the first (if not the first) cars to be known as a "compact" car. It was defined as a rather small car with a reasonable amount of class in the trim department. It was not a cheap, entry-level, "strippo" car with little more than a body, a steering wheel, seats, and an engine barely strong enough to power a lawnmower. The Rambler pioneered a number of interesting marketing concepts. It was a personal, "around town" car rather than what had been the traditional "highway" car in which to take the family on long vacations. It was pitched in ads to the emerging middle class and the upper-class lady drivers and housewives.

The underlying suggestion was to buy a Rambler as a second car. The new idea caught on. The darling Rambler produced a need for a house with an attached two-car garage in the growing American suburbs. Despite the 1958 song "Beep Beep" that told the story of a mighty Cadillac being passed at nearly 100 miles per hour by a little Nash Rambler stuck in second gear, the charming Rambler set the stage for a corporate direction at the new American Motors that would be an Achilles heel by the early 1960s. The direction American Motors was headed was an admirable one—producing efficient cars to reduce consumption of precious fossil fuel. And for a while, AMC sold a lot of cars based on solid construction, reliability, and economy of operation.

But even before it really got started, that message began to fade slightly with the introduction of the 1949 overhead valve (OHV) Oldsmobile "Rocket" V-8 engine. This legendary new engine whetted the appetite of the American buying public for power and speed. Chrysler introduced the "Hemi" V-8 in 1951, and though it was only 331 ci, it was a large-displacement engine for the time. The growing power race was stoked by circle track racing of genuine stock cars during the formative years of NASCAR (National Association for Stock Car Automobile Racing). The "race on Sunday, sell on Monday" marketing philosophy was embraced by carmakers from the efforts of amateur racers, and that philosophy sold new cars.

By 1955 the most mass-produced, high-revving small-block V-8 in automotive history hit the marketplace in the new 1955 Chevrolets. The 265-ci V-8 was lightweight, compact, and of a clean and simple design. It gave the Chevrolet line the image of power and prestige that is with us today. Chrysler upped the ante with the introduction of the 1955 Chrysler 300. It was in the first in the series of high-performance "letter" cars that has continued with the 2000 Chrysler 300M. The 1955 Chrysler 300 must be considered the first true factory musclecar. It was distinctive enough from the regular Chrysler line to be recognized on the street as a "factory hot rod" and sported a 331-ci Hemi V-8 with a racing camshaft, dual four barrels, and it produced an incredible 300 brake horsepower. The 300 had special suspension to handle the power output and the hefty weight of the 4,005-pound car.

The 1949 135-brake horsepower 303.7-ci Rocket 88 Olds may be the great-grandfather of the postwar super cars, but Chevrolet hit a grand slam with the 1955 Chevrolet and the 162-brake horsepower 265-ci V-8.

AMC dealers were busy trying to sell under-powered, glitzy barges and gas-sipping compact cars, both with outdated engines under the hoods in 1955. There was only one bright spot at American Motors: the first true American musclecar, the 1957 Rambler Rebel, was unveiled. It came from American Motors seven years before the fabled Pontiac GTO.

Having no V-8 of its own, AMC bought a 320/352-ci, 208/220-brake horsepower V-8 from Packard. This somewhat outdated OHV motor was fitted to the engine bay of the 1955 and 1956 Ambassador models. That tipped the scales at up to 3,800 pounds. With the Big Three all having new lighter weight OHV V-8s with as much as 300 brake horsepower by 1955, Nash had fallen behind in what was becoming a horsepower race. The big Nashes and the Rambler line plodded along with six cylinders. They were good engines, but certainly were not speed demons. The new American Motors Corporation was pushing comfort, ride, styling, and economical-to-buy-and-drive cars. The cars were not lighting the American buying public's fire, and sales were far and few between for dealers.

The company finally designed and produced an all-new, all-AMC V-8 with 250 ci and 190 brake horsepower for 1956. For 1957 this motor became 327 ci and 255 brake horsepower. Meant for the Ambassador line, the 327 was dropped into a special model of the compact 1957 Rambler that used unibody construction. This little Rambler was a four-door hardtop. A limited production of 1,500 cars was produced in a special light silver-gray metallic with a bronze/gold spear down the sides. The car was offered with a Hydra-matic automatic transmission that had good acceleration, but the car became a real factory hot rod with a three-speed manual transmission and overdrive. The 1957 Rambler, called the "Rebel," was the second-fastest American production car. Only the fuel-injected 1957 Corvette was faster than the Rambler. It should be noted that the Rebel with the three-speed and overdrive did have a 4.10:1 ring and pinion that added a lot of zip off the line.

The Rebel made a big impression on the motoring press of the time and should be honored as being what the history revisionists of today tout the later 1964 GTO—the first American musclecar. Many say the LeMans-based GTO was the first compact car to have a large V-8 engine (usually defined as more than 300 ci). But that widely accepted definition ignores the fact that American Motors accomplished that feat with the 1957

Why don't we enter high-performance Rambler V-8s in racing?

BECAUSE THE ONLY RACE RAMBLER CARES ABOUT IS THE HUMAN RACE!

Racing has a real fascination as professional drivers unleash raw horsepower and flaunt death. It's a thrilling sport—in the right place.

Out of its proper place, racing is deadly. Yet there are those who are glamorizing and advertising race-track speeds in order to sell cars.

This is not in the public interest, and Rambler will have no part in it.

Glorification of horsepower tempts teen-agers to think high-speed driving is 'in'—and safety 'out'—makes irresponsible drivers even more irresponsible, contributes to the mounting carnage on the nation's highways.

> **IMPORTANT NOTE:**
>
> Rambler is strongly in favor of responsive horsepower and performance—offers engines up to 270 HP. But we are strongly against glamorizing raw horsepower and speed to the point where irresponsible drivers may be tempted to abuse them. We believe automobiles should have the best of both—a sensible and satisfying balance of performance and economy, as well as roominess and handling ease. That's the way we build Ramblers.

While many people are still apathetic, growing numbers are joining Rambler's crusade against the promotion of excessive speed and horsepower.

Are Ramblers underpowered? Emphatically not! Every Rambler delivers spirited performance. Our Ambassador, for instance, offers a 270-hp V-8. It would be no trick at all to beef up that rating to 300-hp or more. *But it would serve you no better.*

Rambler's prime concern is for your safety, comfort, satisfaction, and savings.

That's why every Rambler balances turnpike performance with sensible economy.

It's why Rambler gives you *Advanced Unit Construction, Double-Safety Brakes* (separate systems, front and rear); a *Ceramic-Armored exhaust system* that protects against rust and fume leaks. Plus optional headrests that act as headguards against whiplash if your car is struck from behind.

Rambler spends millions on testing cars *before* they go on sale, millions more on safety advances. *But not one cent to glorify speed.*

We welcome your comments, and invite you to join our crusade for safe motoring. *American Motors Corporation, Detroit 32, Michigan.*

No. 1 in Usefulness to the User

RAMBLER
American · Classic V-8 or 6 · Ambassador V-8

RAMBLER CLASSIC 770 HARDTOP

This ad crystalized Rambler's philosophy on organized closed-course racing as well as steet racing. The company went against the musclecar trend and instead focused on family cars.

Rebel seven years earlier. The 1955 Chrysler 300 may have been America's first true factory "hot rod," but the 1957 Rebel was America's first true sedan-style musclecar. And you can take that to the (historical) bank.

Sadly, the little Rebel was a flash-in-the-pan at AMC. A recession hit the country in 1958 and small, economical cars began to sell well for AMC. The big-wheelbase Nash Ambassador series was eliminated after 1957, and all 1958 Ambassadors were constructed using the 108-inch Rambler platform. Even the Nash name died in 1957. The four-barrel, 250-brake horsepower 327-ci V-8 continued, but the new 270-brake horsepower version of the 327 was only offered in the cruiser-style Ambassador. The performance concept of the 1957 327 V-8 Rebels was also gone by 1958, and so was the magic the car produced.

As the youth of America fell seriously in love with 409 V-8 Chevrolets, 406 Fords, and 413 Dodges in the early 1960s, AMC came out with an antiracing ad campaign in 1964 that was really a head-in-the-sand, antiperformance message. All across the country, Saturday-night stoplight drag racing made High Noon gunslingers out of every crew cut or ducktailed teenager in America. The "race on Sunday" at the track theme was moved to the streets. The emerging American performance car became the measure of manhood to young buyers, and kids lusted for the crown jewels of ego, a 409 Chevy Impala or a 421 Tri-Power Catalina. And they had to have a four-speed with George Hurst's shifter on the floor. American streets roared with loud pipes, screamed with squealing tires, and no kid got more than a couple thousand miles out of a set of tires, but they didn't care.

At AMC, the ads were for the darling Rambler American winning the Mobile Gas Economy Runs, the Olympics of Gas Sipping. Those over 50 years old were the only ones paying attention. The increase of total cars sold in the United States grew so much that AMC had its golden years of sales from 1958 to 1965. The cars set sales records and made money at AMC, yet AMC's total market share of the American new car market was always less than 5 percent—and slipping. GM, Chrysler, and Ford were into building hot street cars and sponsoring racing in a big way to impress the young car buyers who bought the cars. Young buyers also influenced their friends and families on what brands to buy, even if they bought sedate sedans. Brand loyalty was a badge of honor worn with major pride. The "Big Three" poured money into drag racing, NASCAR track racing, and road racing to promote the sales of cars that did (illegal)

street racing. It was the age of Tire Smoke. Peeling out was the true measure of a man. Laying the longest patch of rubber going out of a drive-in restaurant elevated your peer group social status. (Though it annoyed the heck out of the neighbors and honked off the cops.)

A custom 1932 Ford Highboy with a flathead V-8 sporting Ardun heads, Edelbrock intake, and Stromberg 97 carbs was king in the 1950s, but a factory-built, huge-cubic-inch, overhead-valve V-8 performance car was the golden idol 1960s teenagers worshiped. "She's real fine, my 409" was the new Battle Hymn of the Republic. All this time, AMC stood its ground and made cars that were sensible and economical. The 327 AMC V-8 was an outdated stone by 1965. Because AMC shunned performance and racing, the aftermarket cam, tube header, and intake manifold companies never made anything bolt-on, off-the-shelf for the AMC 327. Plus, it was a 1955 design that just didn't lend itself to high-performance applications.

Hence, new 1965 Marlins were underpowered Rambler Classic fastbacks that wouldn't even chirp a skinny, bias-belted, 6.95x14 tire on the one-two shift. Kids shunned Rambler dealers as if one could get leprosy if you entered a showroom. Many AMC dealers were located in old downtown buildings that formerly housed turn-of-the-century cable cars and were staffed with salesmen that would make Mel Brooks' 2,000-year-old man look like a teenager. Or else the dealerships were located in rural areas where Ramblers, Farmall tractors, and seed corn were sold off the same sales floor.

AMC cars were stereotyped as Ramblers and the once proud name became a put-down of antiquated automobiles. The 1964-1/2 Mustang hit the pavement in droves, and the AMC boys on Plymouth Road in Detroit began to see their automotive careers flash before their eyes. GTOs roamed Woodward Avenue and the little old lady from Pasadena ruled Colorado Boulevard in her new, shiny red Super Stock Dodge. Rambler sales were so great in the first half of the sixties that the lines on the wall chart resembled the dive-bomber pattern of a World War II B-25. AMC management began to realize they had missed the boat. A huge explosion in fun, styling, and performance had occurred while they were down in the basement vaults counting penny profits from pre-1965 sales. With terror in their hearts, Dick Teague and his styling department, and engine designer Dave Potter, both with budgets barely enough to buy the whole staff lunch at McDonald's, set out to play catch-up for American Motors to the Big Three. And what a ride it was to be!

two

Rambler Becomes American Motors
Staving Off Bankruptcy

AMC was in trouble by 1965. Company stock was losing ground as sales started to go downhill. The press was watching Studebaker go bankrupt and was predicting that American Motors would quickly follow. The crest of the compact car wave was crashing on the beach, rinsing the tires of the invading creatures called Bugs and Toyopets from Germany and Japan.

The Rambler American, the bread and butter of the company, now had booming import competition as well as homegrown rivals such as the Ford Falcon, Chevy II, and Pontiac Tempest. All hopes of stemming the outflow of ledger red ink were pinned on one man and his department: Richard A. Teague and his Advanced Styling Studios on Plymouth Road in Detroit.

The Tarpon

Teague said he lived in the smallest house in Bloomfield Hills, Michigan, where a lot of Detroit auto executives resided. His three children went to school with other auto executives' kids, and his wife shopped at the same grocery store where the executives' wives shopped. Scuttlebutt about trends in the new car market was always out there. Teague was a wise man, and he had to have some clues as to what Ford, GM, and Chrysler were up to in their styling departments. He also had a good idea what the market wanted.

Teague loved pre–World War II cars. He had a passion for taking old styling and making it new again. He saw the resurgence of the fastback starting with the 1963-1/2 Ford Galaxy 500 XL and the 1963 Corvette split-window coupe. The roofline on these cars resembled the cabin speedsters of the late 1920s that looked like wooden power boats with wheels. That styling was refined with the 1942 Chevrolet aerosedan, the first car that could be truly considered a fastback. Torpedo-back styling, as it came to be called, faded with the advent of the two-door hardtop in 1949.

The 1964 Rambler American Tarpon fastback could have changed the course of history for American Motors had it been made instead of the larger 1965 Rambler Classic Marlin.
Larry Mitchell collection

Early 1964 Advanced Styling Studio drawings show the extreme fastback styling and the unique "Ramble" seat that evolved into the 1966 Vignale AMX prototype. Larry Mitchell collection

Everything old is new again and Teague had an ace up his sleeve for AMC. It was called the Tarpon. This was an AMC fastback fish to swim in waters with the new Plymouth Barracuda fastback. This styling concept arrived just in time to watch the stunning new 1964-1/2 Mustang take the car market by storm and create a new American class of cars called "pony cars." Teague had to know a fastback for the Mustang was coming by 1965. Why else would he and his crew graft a fastback roofline to his cute, restyled 1964 American?

The 1964 Rambler Tarpon show car was simply drop-dead gorgeous. It looked like an updated Auburn boattail speedster. The car was shown at the SAE (Society of Automotive Engineers) convention in January 1964. Just like the new Mustang, the car carried the 2+2 moniker, which meant two people could be seated in the front bucket seats and two in the rear on the bench seat. Teague and his small band of merry styling men had something in the hopper for AMC's entry into the new youth market.

The high-performance craze was sweeping the nation and was fueled by teenage baby boomers with the hots for neat, new, high-performance personal cars. The little deuce coupe was out and the little GTO was in. And the Ford Mustang set sales records that have never been equaled.

When Teague and his wife, Marian, went to Europe on vacation, AMC President Roy Abernethy took Teague's darling Tarpon and made a whale out of it. Abernethy never liked little cars and made the decision to place the Tarpon's new fastback roofline on the larger Rambler Classic. The result was the 1965 Marlin. And so yet another fish took up residence in the ocean of cars. Teague never said anything bad about anyone, but one could sense he was disappointed in AMC's top management for upsizing the American-based Tarpon to the larger Classic-based Marlin. A unique body style (comparable to the 1964 1/2 Mustang) was gone. AMC sold only 10,327 Marlins.

Some historians might say Abernethy had little choice. The Mustang had a small-block 260/289-ci V-8 that slipped right into the engine bay of the little pony car. The AMC 287/327-ci V-8 was far too large and heavy for the bay of the American, and there was no V-8 driveline available for the American either. And performance potential for the outdated AMC motor was severely limited.

AMC Engineer Dave Potter had a new, thin-wall, medium-block 290 V-8 in the works, but it was at least a year away. Abernethy probably suspected luxury cars such as the 1965 Pontiac Catalina 2+2 were coming from GM. With no V-8 for the American, the Marlin had to be targeted for

The 1965 AMX (I) pushmobile first shown in January 1966 at the SAE Convention in Cobo Hall, Detroit. Larry Mitchell collection

This 1966 Vignale AMX is on the Project IV Tour in the summer of 1966. The fully operational, steel-bodied AMX prototype was handmade by Vignale in Italy. *Larry Mitchell collection*

The dusty interior of the Vignale AMX is pictured as it sits on display at the Museum of Speed at the Talledaga Speedway in Alabama. One rear seat is folded down, allowing access to the rear Ramble seat. *Bob Kenworthy*

the higher end of the market. No matter what anyone knew, no one could have really predicted that the Marlin was going to be such a poor seller, but it was. The youth market wanted nimble, Mustang-type personal-sports cars. The Marlin was just too big, too underpowered, and stuck with an outdated torque-tube rear drive. Everyone knew what the Mustang was, but no one knew about the Marlin. The over-30 Rambler buyers shunned it and so did the under-30 baby boomers.

Teague's Advanced Styling Studios at AMC had other irons in the fire. Behind the closed doors lurked drawings, clay mock-ups, and fiberglass concept vehicles. These ideas had such names on them as Mach 1, Demon, Rebel, Rogue, and even AMX for American Motors Xperimental. The future of American Motors rested with these cars, more than many knew at the time. These drawings and concepts came together in what was to be called Project IV.

A Bold New Direction— The Project IV Concept Cars

In 1965, AMC Styling Studio ideas came together in a group of four different "cars" that were lumped together and called "Project IV." Pushmobile fiberglass mock-ups were made of the four cars and trimmed out for a proposed public display to test market reaction. These concept cars were in addition to the bold new styling planned for the production Ambassador and the Classic (renamed the Rebel) for the fall of 1966 as all-new 1967 models.

One pushmobile featured an aggressive 2+2 style with a unique rumble seat called the Ramble seat, and it carried the name AMX. It was finished before the other units and shown at the SAE convention in Detroit's Cobo Hall in January 1966. The car was well received by the convention attendees and the automotive press. Immediately, AMC's top management decided to have a running car hand-built out of steel and contracted with Vignale in Turin, Italy. Vignale employed old-world "panel-beater" craftsmen who had the skill to create just about anything on four wheels.

The fully operational car was completed in under three months and delivered to AMC's Plymouth Road headquarters. It arrived in Detroit just in time to go on the Project IV U.S. tour in selected major cities including Milwaukee, mainly for AMC employees in Milwaukee and Kenosha. The event was by invitation for local AMC dealers, businessmen, and financiers. The "Vignale" AMX was the only real, running car in the Project IV group; the rest were fiberglass shells with no interiors or drivelines.

The following was printed on the special green invitation for the Project IV showings:

"AMX. A cantilever roof with integral roll bar and the 'Ramble seat' are among unique features of the AMX. The experimental model is powered by American Motors' all-new 290 cubic-inch V-8, has a 'four-on-the-floor' console transmission. In addition to the 'Ramble seat,' this prototype has fold-down contoured rear seats.

"Cavalier. An experimental subcompact design, with interchangeable body panels which sharply reduces tooling costs. Right front and left rear fenders are identical, as are their opposites. Hood, deck lid are identical. The four doors could be stamped from two die sets. Yet grille and rear-end treatments and positioning of the roof give the front and rear strikingly different appearances.

"AMX II. This modified AMX II fastback features a 'V' rear window to blend with rear deck contours. Safety taillights with green, amber and red lenses would give cars behind immediate indication of the driver's intentions or actions. Doors would lock automatically when the ignition key is turned on.

"Vixen. A deeply recessed concave rear window flowing into the deck highlights this Vixen sports model. Because of this non-reflective shape and position, the glass appears to be invisible from both inside and outside. Vents on the landau-type roof side panels are angled at 45 degrees to give the driver wider rear vision."

It is somewhat difficult to trace the origins of AMC Styling Studio drawings, clay mock-ups, and

The 1966 Project IV Cavalier concept vehicle became the restyled Rambler American, which was renamed the Hornet in 1970. Larry Mitchell collection

The AMX II was another 1966 Project IV, nonoperational concept car that evolved into the 1968 Javelin. Many features of the companion Vignale AMX (I) such as the fastback roofline and grille were transferred onto the AMX II to form the 1968 production Javelin. Larry Mitchell collection

The final 1966 Project IV concept vehicle was the sporty Vixen. It shared the front end with the Cavalier. The rear roofline foretold of the 1973 Hornet hatchback. Larry Mitchell collection

fiberglass shells. From this collective bunch of ideas and experiments, some wound up being dead ends while some became actual production models a few years later. Some concept car names were never used by AMC while some models, including the Demon, were used by other companies.

Rogue and Rebel were names printed on various drawings and were real pushmobiles, but those names wound up on completely different AMC production cars. The roofline of one mock-up might have become the real roof on a very different production car a few years later. On the other hand, retracing some of the history is very easy.

The real Vignale-running AMX can be traced back to two fiberglass mock-ups. The first was created on a 1964 Rambler American platform.

Originally, the vehicle was not built as a running car and didn't have an interior. However, it was eventually fitted with a drivetrain and a 1968 Javelin interior. Teague called that vehicle a "styling buck."

The second AMX (I) was a fiberglass shell on wheels, and it was the one shown early in 1966 at the SAE convention. The steel-bodied Vignale AMX was produced after the second AMX (I) pushmobile. All this took place in late 1965 and into 1966. It is interesting to note that the Vignale AMX was not a two-seat sports car, but it had small jump seats in the rear and the Ramble seat, also. It was a genuine 2+2 or four-passenger concept car.

Styling Studio artists Bob Nixon, Erich Kugler, and Fred Hudson created or collaborated on

The Vignale AMX had the new-for-1966 AMC 290 V-8 under the hood. It is shown here with the Ramble seat closed. This car was the forerunner of the 1968 AMX, but was a 2+2, not a two-seater. Larry Mitchell collection

Shown for the first time, this rare photograph shows one of the Dow Smith resin AMX I bodies being stress tested. Note from the shape of the door, it was molded from the Vignale AMX. Larry Mitchell collection

This 1967 concept car named the AMX III foretold of the coming 1968 Javelin production car as a possible station wagon. The idea never came to fruition, but the rear end became the 1971 Hornet Sportabout. Larry Mitchell collection

numerous AMX vehicle drawings over time under the direct supervision of Teague. The original idea of a two-passenger-only, high-performance sports car was shelved until the new chairman of the board, Robert Evans, gave the project life in the fall of 1966.

The AMX II took on more importance after the Project IV tour was over, because the project leading to the 1968 Javelin was approved in late spring of 1966. The eventual 1968 Javelin shape came directly from the AMX II, but the AMX 2 and Demon drawings provided a great influence. The AMX 2 and Demon featured fastback rooflines that the more formal coupe-looking concepts Rebel and Rogue did not have. This demonstrates the blurring of ideas, drawings, and pushmobiles that the basis of both the 1968 Javelin and the 1968 AMX. The original AMX styling buck, the second pushmobile, and the Vignale AMX all are with us today. However, the AMX II shell was dumpsterized in 1967.

The Vixen and the Cavalier concept cars were combined and refined in 1970. They replaced the Rambler American as the new Hornet. The American didn't die as some may think; it was reborn as the Hornet. The 1970 Hornet sedan body can easily be seen by covering up the roofline of the Vixen. Take away the blackout area of the rear window, and the fastback lines of the upper rear quarter panel of the Vixen become the 1973 Hornet hatchback. For the historical records, the 1970 Hornet gave rise to the 1970-1/2 Gremlin. Both the Vixen and the Cavalier became chainsaw fodder.

Additional AMX Design Exercises

When the decision to make the 1968 AMX was approved by September 1966, the idea to make it in resin crossed AMC Engineering's mind. A "plastic" body might be more cost effective, a Corvette-type selling point for the car, and the car could be rushed into production sooner.

Teague contracted with Dow Smith, Inc., in Detroit to produce two, one-piece resin bodies for evaluation. The bodies were like life-size slot car bodies and were to be mounted on a steel platform if the project went ahead. Dow Smith subjected one body to torsional twist testing while the AMC Styling Studios trimmed out the other to get an idea of how it would look. The trimmed-out body wore a badge on the front fenders that read "AMX 2." Under testing, the body failed to meet required safety and durability standards, and the idea of a plastic-bodied AMX was given up as not practical.

In the spring of 1967, the AMX III concept car was first shown at Chicago and New York auto

The 1968 AMX GT show car grafted a kammback rear end to a 1968 AMX to create a unique and aggressive coupe. The chopped-off rear end was used on the 1970 Hornet to create the 1970-1/2 Gremlin. Larry Mitchell collection

shows. Its looks forecasted the 1968 Javelin production car but with a station wagon rear end. It could easily be called a Javelin station wagon, but it came a year before the 1968 Javelin. The rear of this concept car, combined with the final production front end of the 1970 Hornet, was incorporated into the 1971 Sportabout wagon design.

In the spring of 1968, a unique AMC-styling exercise, called the AMX GT, was displayed at the New York auto show. The bright, Candy Apple Red car featured a 1968 AMX front end with a chopped-off rear end that was known as a kammback. The car had a fierce look and resembled an early altered Bonneville-type, speedrun car, especially with the Laker sidepipes and pancake "Moon" wheel discs. The shape for the 1970-1/2 Gremlin, the ram-air hood scoop for the 1970 AMX, and Javelin hood was lifted from this car.

Wearing an AMC Wisconsin Manufacturer's license plate is what appears to be a 1969 AMX (hooded dash overlay) with a bizarre rear-end treatment using stock 1969 Rambler American taillights and rear bumper. Nothing is currently known about this car. Larry Mitchell collection

AMC Engines

The heart of any performance car is its engine. It is the biggest part of a car an enthusiast is concerned about—especially back in the days of the early American musclecar.

The Rambler family of V-8s from 1956 to 1966 were the 250/287/327-ci V-8s. They were good motors for passenger-car use, but were not suited for hot rodding. When American Motors announced to the world that it was against racing and high performance in 1964, no aftermarket manufacturer made any hop-up parts for Rambler engines. For performance use, these engines were outdated and were passed up with the dawn of the "big blocks" in the early 1960s. AMC knew it, which is one reason why they came out with that ad in the first place.

It was a simple cop-out and a major marketing mistake. Ramblers were branded by the new youth market as granny cars, and AMC management thought they could continue to make a living from that narrow slice of the new car pie with its outdated motors. But they were wrong and corporate gross profits went into red ink by 1965.

In a desperate attempt to update the engines, AMC engineer Dave Potter and his crew designed a new family of AMC V-8s that were modern, using thin-wall casting techniques. As in the Rambler tradition, the motors (V-8s and I-6s) were not garden-variety cast, but they contained a high nickel content making a hard and durable alloy casting. Both the blocks and the heads are alloy, making all the AMC engines ever made the finest material-quality produced by a carmaker.

The first of these new engines was the 1966 290-ci V-8, introduced in the 1966-1/2 Rogue, but available in the entire American line for the year. It was a 100 percent American Motors engine but used Delco ignition, purchased from General Motors for simple convenience and cost considerations. The distributor was up front, for easy maintenance. Combustion chambers were wedge-shaped, while the connecting rods and the crankshaft were cast, malleable iron. Horsepower was 200 with a two-barrel carb and 225 with a four-barrel and single exhaust. The engines were externally balanced for exceptional smoothness.

Because of the design and the light, internal reciprocating mass, the AMC engines produced abundant torque compared to the Chevy and Ford engines of the same displacement. The block had room to grow and became the 343-ci V-8 for 1967. Both the 290 and the 343 were called the "Typhoon" V-8s. AMC had plans to produce a 390-ci version for the 1968 passenger car line and it was meant to be a high-torque, trailer-towing option for the Ambassador—at first. By 1967, AMC reversed its antiperformance attitude and set out to create a performance image. The new 390 V-8 was badly needed to establish some credibility for AMC's new performance image, so it was named the "AMX 390" and premiered in the new, 1968-1/2 AMX sports car. This engine was the creme de la creme as it featured forged rods and crankshaft, some things only found in special, racing high-performance motors from GM, Ford, and Chrysler. But, one can never forget, it was not a race-bred engine brought to the streets like a Chrysler 426 Hemi, 427 Chevrolet, or 429 Ford.

The new AMC family of V-8s, from 1966 to the end, powered passenger cars until 1979 and Jeeps until 1991. Sizes were 290, 304, 343, 360, 390, and 401 ci. Each engine shared the same basic external dimensions, although they differed inside in many areas. The last year for the 401 in passenger cars was 1974. Chrysler liked the AMC 360 V-8 so well that it continued to use it in the Grand Cherokees until 1991.

The 1968 AMX 390 was a medium-sized block rated at 315 brake horsepower at 4,600 rpm and "big block" torque of 425 pounds-feet at only 3,200 rpm. It was this excellent torque characteristic and the non-big-block size that made the AMC 390 V-8 a powerhouse in the musclecars the company made.

Since it weighed less than 600 pounds, the AMC performance cars—especially the AMX two-seater—were not nearly as nose-heavy as cars such as the 396 Camaro, the 428 Mustang, or the worst of all: the Hemi 'Cuda. Those engines tipped the scales at between 750 and 850 pounds. The AMC cars had big-block torque and very good overall handling because they weren't so nose-heavy.

Racing improvements made the AMC V-8s even better. In 1970 the dogleg or "d-port" exhaust port developed by AMC engineers for the Trans-Am race car engines in 1969 became a standard feature of all the AMC V-8s. These heads in stock format could outflow a comparable Chevy V-8 head that was mildly ported and polished. In 1971, when compression was on its way down and performance with it, AMC engineers made a set of stock exhaust manifolds that were patterned after the stock street Hemi units from Chrysler, and the AMC engines experienced a noticeable performance increase again. By 1972, an AMC 401 V-8 in a Javelin could whip up on a 455 Firebird or a 454 Chevelle stock versus stock with similar options and gearing, all because of the dogleg heads and the "free-flow" exhaust manifolds.

An AMX 390 V-8 is endurance tested in the dyno room at the AMC engine plant in Kenosha, Wisconsin, in 1968. Larry Mitchell collection

The 1970 AMC 390 became the 401 for 1971 because AMC needed the image of an over-400-ci V-8—"401" sounded bigger and badder than "390." The slightly longer stroke reduced emissions, something the federal government was demanding. All 401s had forged rods and cranks like the 390. All 360-ci and under engines used cast-iron cranks and rods. The 343/390 and 360/401 heads were identical in their respective years, while 290/304 heads were the same castings as the larger engines, but used small valves for fuel economy. Basically, all exhaust manifolds were the same in respective years with minor exceptions.

Today, the expertise to rebuild AMC V-8s has been lost except to a handful of builders in the United States and Canada. Most general automotive shops will rebuild them to Chevrolet specs and the engines will not hold proper oil pressure, run well, or last long. AMC engines must be rebuilt to AMC Shop Manual specs, after which they are excellent performers. Further details on rebuilding AMC V-8s can be obtained from selected AMC hobby sources, including AMX Enterprises in Arvada, Colorado.

Final tips on AMC V-8s: When rebuilding, hold main and rod bearings to between .001 and .0015-inch; replace the front timing cover with a brand-new (not rebuilt) one obtained from Chrysler or Jeep parts suppliers, because 25–35-year-old covers are worn out in the oil pump cavity and will drop oil pressure even with new gears; overbore if taper in the block exceeds .005-inch in any cylinder and totally rebalance the entire reciprocating assembly, including the pistons, rods, crank, harmonic balancer, and flywheel/flexplate if any of these items is changed out for another unit(s), new or from another engine. AMC V-8s are "Detroit," or externally balanced, and these parts do not interchange, even between motors of the same displacement and year. They fit, but the swap causes the engine to be imbalanced and it will shake itself to death in short order. When in doubt on a rebuild, spend the money to professionally rebalance the entire motor.

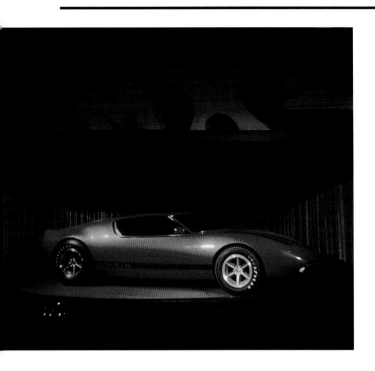

The AMX/ 2 pushmobile on display at the 1969 Chicago Auto Show. More than any other, this sleek, midengined, Italian-looking AMC show-shell turned heads and got people talking about the new image of American Motors. Larry Mitchell

When the AMC Kenosha plant was shutting down in 1987, a plant worker found a few black and white slides in an envelope in the bottom of his toolbox. Prints were made and a car came to life that history knew nothing about. The former AMC worker remembers nothing much about the car except he had a minor role in creating it from a 1968–69 production-line AMX. It was done at the Kenosha plant, but for reasons he does not recall.

The car is the AMX with modified rear quarter panels and a rear trim panel, taillights, and rear bumper from a production Rambler American. It appears the trunk lid is not hinged and does not open.

The 1969 fiberglass-bodied AMX/2 is not to be confused with a 1965–66 drawing with the name AMX 2. The AMX/2, an AMC-styling studio extension of the 1966 Vignale AMX, was a low-slung, two-passenger, ultra-high-performance, mid-engined Ferrari wannabe. Teague personally owned a 1963 Ferrari Type 250 GT Berlinetta coupe and always had a love for the marque's styling.

The tangerine-fading-into-red pushmobile was shown around the auto show circuit in 1969 and created quite a stir. It also helped to crystalize the public's new image of AMC as a performance-oriented, progressive carmaker with a future. There was no information about the car at the shows. The AMC people at the display would only say when asked about the car, "Who knows?" From the three or four AMX/2 show shells came the 1970-1/2 AMX/3 discussed in the AMX chapter.

Reversal of Philosophy

AMC was going through a transition in 1966. The decline in sales was the start of a change in corporate philosophy. The old antiperformance attitude of 1964, which delayed AMC's entry into the new youth market, was weakening. In an effort to attract some young buyers into the dealers' showrooms, the Marlin, Ambassador, and Classic got a new four-speed manual shift transmission from Warner Gear, a division of Borg Warner. A very attractive chrome-ribbed console with optional center fold-down armrest went in between the beautiful and comfortable Strato-Lounger bucket seats with stainless-steel trim. On the dash was an optional dealer-installed tachometer for all the world to see. It redlined at 5,000 rpm, a frightening speed for the 1950s-designed AMC V-8. Can you imagine pulling up next to a new 1966 426 Hemi Dodge Charger at a stoplight with your top-of-the-line AMC 327 V-8 Marlin with a four-speed and outfitted with that intimidating dash tach the size of a 6-ounce can of Ocean Spray cranberry sauce? I get chills just thinking about it.

To be fair, a very few progressive Rambler dealers tried to race a 1964 or 1965 Ambassador or Classic to gain some respect for the brand. One lone 1964 Ambassador tried to run in a few NASCAR races, but the car never had a chance. Kraft Rambler ran an Ambassador at the local drag strips and it was at least not a complete embarrassment.

The new upper management at AMC realized the once proud Rambler name had a negative meaning in the youth market. However, it still had positive meaning to a bread-and-butter older market and the dealers that had Rambler in their business names. The Rambler name began to slowly fade with the removal of the name from the Marlin for 1966. The name Classic was no longer considered a positive factor, and the 1966 Rambler Classic two-door hardtop became the "Rebel," a name seen in the AMC styling studios on drawings and a mock-up that had nothing to do with the real 1966 Classic model. The process would continue for the next three years in a low-key campaign across the United States and Canada. It was the closing of an era, and the winds of change blew down the corridors of American Motors corporate headquarters.

The AMX/2 was the wildest idea and the most exotic concept ever to come from AMC Vice President Dick Teague's Advanced Styling Studios. Thought to be a pet project of Teague's, it led to the 1970-1/2 AMX/3. Larry Mitchell collection

The 1966-1/2 Sun Gold and Classic Black Rogue was created to showcase the new 1966 290-ci AMC V-8. The car was AMC's first attempt at selling the youth market a Mustang-type performance car. Larry Mitchell collection

The 1966-1/2 Rogue V-8

Dave Potter was an engine man who came from Willys and had designed the 1956 AMC 250/287/327 family of V-8s. By 1965, he was working on a new family of AMC engines that put the company in the same league as the Big Three. In 1966, the new V-8s featured new thinwall construction techniques. This V-8 engine and its offspring are covered in a sidebar in this chapter. At first, it was only 290 ci and 225 brake horsepower with a four-barrel, but it was lighter, revved faster, and had hot rodding potential far and above the V-8s it replaced.

To introduce this new motor to the public, AMC had to have a Mustang equal, at least in size. The 1966 Rambler American two-door hardtop was chosen, and a very special version was created. The unibody was beefed up to handle the extra power of the V-8. A stronger driveline was created, a stiffer suspension, and disc brakes were made available A front sway bar was added, as well as bigger tires and rims.

On the inside, the highline interior was installed. It consisted of the excellent Strato-Lounger buckets with stainless-steel trim, and a full console for the cars built with Flash-o-matic (Warner Gear) automatic transmissions. A four-speed transmission was fitted to the new 290 V-8, but no console was offered for the Ford-built shifter sticking out of the floor. A center fold-down armrest and bolster combination was optional. The interior of this special model was all black vinyl.

On the outside, the previous designation "440" was replaced with a new script "Rogue" emblem. It came right from a fiberglass mock-up of a concept car that actually developed into the Javelin. These new Rogues were painted a striking color combination of Sun Gold metallic with Classic Black on the roof and the trunk lid. AMC built 1,700 of them, one for each AMC dealer in the United States and Canada. Most were 290, four-barrel, single-exhaust cars with four-speed transmission, center armrest, power drum brakes, and an open 3.15:1 rear axle.

The 1966-1/2 Rogues showcased the new 290 V-8. After the first 1,700 special Rogues were built, the AMC customer could order a Rogue and outfit it using the option list. Solar Yellow and Classic Black was a popular color combination. The V-8 Rogue wasn't a Mustang beater, but it received excellent press and started to show the world AMC had some life left. *Motor Trend* tested a Rogue and only got a 17.6-second quarter-mile time with the four-speed, but they could tell the car had potential. In 1966, 8,718 total Rogues were built, including the 1,700 specials.

The 1967-1/2 Super-Americans

In December 1967, an ad appeared in selected national car magazines. It announced that American Motors dealers were selling any 1967 Rambler American, except a station wagon, with the new 280-brake horsepower, four-barrel 343 V-8, which was a new version of the 290 V-8. This was earth-shaking news. Imagine AMC making an American as a direct answer to Chevrolet stuffing an RPO L30, 275-brake horsepower 327 V-8 in the 1967 Chevy II Nova Super Sport. Wow! Finally, AMC offered a musclecar. While some AMC dealers loved it, many were appalled and never tried to sell the 343 V-8 cars AMC called the Super-Americans. Many AMC dealers were still choking over the new 1967 Ambassadors and Rebels that looked as if they were styled by General Motors.

Wild as it was, few 343 V-8 Super-Americans were ever sold. Virtually no dealers ordered any for stock; the cars were built to order for the handful of young buyers. Many Rambler dealers felt these factory hot rods would scare off Ma and Pa Kettle, and it was the older clientele that kept the dealerships going by buying a grass-green four-door six-cylinder American with an optional automatic transmission. Few dealers even wanted any under-30 "kids" coming in and trying to talk to their sales staff, who had a combined age equal to moon rocks. And they had about the same savvy when it came to cams, headers, and Holley carbs.

AMC made mistakes with the Super-Americans. The car came with an engine rated at 280 brake horsepower, but sporting a single exhaust pipe the size of a chicken neck. The American unibody was really not strong enough to stand the high amount of torque the 343 put out and body twist was a problem. Hardtops with the 343 V-8 would crack windshields due to excessive body flex.

An AMC dealer in Rockford, Illinois, bought a 1967 Super-American for show-and-tell at local drag races, but bought the two-door sedan, which had a stronger roof. The car did well at the strip in

In December 1967, AMC finally produced serious performance when it dropped the new 280-horsepower 343 V-8 into the two- and four-door sedan and two-door hardtop Rambler American. The engines were coupled to a four-on-the-floor transmission. Larry Mitchell collection

the spring of 1967, but only two other 343 V-8 Americans were sold, one a red two-door sedan, the other a black Rogue hardtop, both four-speeds.

A few other AMC dealers bought 343 Americans, went drag racing, and had moderate success. With new dealer and aftermarket bolt-on performance parts such as headers, cams, and those Holley carbs with a 4.10:1 ring and pinion with slicks, these Super-Americans were the first American Motors cars to dip into the high 12s in the quarter-mile. Randall Rambler of Mesa, Arizona, ran a modified 343 two-door sedan American in the American Hot Rod Association's 6D/SO class where it turned an incredible 12.47 seconds at 116 miles per hour. *Motor Trend* magazine made a project drag racer out of a 343 American and with only minor, bolt-on modifications, ran a best of 13.90 seconds at 100 miles per hour. AMC had entered the world of high performance, but it was nearly a decade late.

three

Javelin 1968–1970

A New Musclecar Challenges the Establishment

The 1968 Javelin was initially approved for production as soon as the final mock-up was completed in April 1966. A number of different roof treatments were considered, including the extreme fastback style of the original Vignale AMX/AMX (I) Project IV mock-up and the more moderate semi-fastback roofline of the AMX II Project IV pushmobile. The AMX (I) roofline sloped all the way back to the rear quarter panel extension cap, and the AMX II roofline had the look of a more formal coupe with the C-pillars blending in with the rear quarter panel long before the rear edge of the panels. As of April 1966, the AMX (I) concept was not going to be made because it had a 2+2 seating arrangement with the Ramble seat, which just didn't seem to be the thing to produce. However, AMC knew it badly needed a car to directly compete with the Mustang and other cars now classed as pony cars.

AMC believed the Javelin needed a little more wheelbase and a little more rear seating room. Some at AMC still liked the idea of up-sizing the Marlin from the Tarpon, even if it didn't sell. The new 1967 Marlin was to be a senior Ambassador with the extreme fastback roof, so a little bigger might be better. By going with a larger pony car than others were making, AMC must have felt it could better sell the car based on slightly larger interior dimensions. (And that became an important point, which the 1968 ads stressed about the car.) The final choice for the basic body was very close to the AMX II.

In the end, the Javelin's only deviation from the AMX II was the grille that became a twin-venturi-style. The rear bumper shape was lifted off the original Vignale AMX, particularly how it wrapped around the side of the rear quarter panels. The sides of the body from the front fenders to the rear quarters were more rounded rather than leaning toward the slab styling and deeply sculpted ridge

The new 1968 Javelin had a grace and beauty about it rarely captured in an automobile. Some might say it was the best-looking pony car of them all. In Matador Red with a white stripe and a black vinyl top, the car was simply handsome.
Larry Mitchell collection

31

Few cars look good as a basic model. This standard Javelin is as plain as they come and still presents an attractive image to the viewer. Larry Mitchell collection

of the two Project IV cars. The rounded "Coke-bottle" panels would be easier to make and the dies would last longer—an important cost consideration. One has to wonder if some stylist at AMC had an inkling of the Coke-bottle styling that was scheduled for the new 1967 Camaro/Firebird.

The roofline became a combination of the AMX (I) and AMX II blended together. Drawings of this combined-roof concept car appeared in June 1966. The object all along was to make a new, fastback sporty pony car using as much of the mechanics and platform from the Rambler American as possible. It cost tens of millions of dollars to bring a totally new car on line, and AMC had to conserve money wherever possible. Making a new car—the Javelin out of the existing Rambler American saved some major expenses.

The final shape of the new Javelin was approved in September 1966. The roofline flowed from the highest portion of the roof directly over the front seatbacks, down at a slight curve, ending above the rear window. An angled dip then gave a French curve effect that gracefully reached out all the way to the rear quarter panel extensions, where it blended in. The quarter panels also rose to

meet the base of the roof. These compound curves—and the long length of the roof base as it met the top of the quarter panel—gave a strong and solid look to the rear of the Javelin when viewed from the sides.

If one were to take a moment to study the shape, it seems artistic magic was created by a small band of stylists that poured forth their souls for the smallest car company in Detroit. The final Javelin looked like nothing else coming from Detroit and was an exciting, clean design. Everything about the lines of the car was attractive and pleasing. To call the car handsome understates the beauty of the new Javelin.

The Javelin name was chosen in a think-tank session at American Motors. Those were the days when the American carmakers fretted over just the right name for new cars. AMC Shows and Exhibits Manager Guy Hadsall Jr. first suggested the name, but it was thought of as being too akin to a weapon. Hadsall argued the positive connotations the name could have—such as the pure sport of Javelin toss in the Olympics. Eventually, the panel agreed and they gave his idea the stamp of approval. So Javelin it was.

By 1967 the market was filled with pony cars. The Mustang had been around since 1964, as had Plymouth's Barracuda. The Chevy Camaro, Pontiac Firebird, and Mercury Cougar were new models for 1967. However, the AMC Javelin was not even the last pony car to hit the showrooms—it was Dodge's 1970 Challenger. And while the Javelin may not have been the biggest seller, it was arguably one of the best-looking in the right colors and trim.

The New Javelin Hits the Showroom

The Javelin was introduced on September 26, 1967, as a new 1968 model. The brochure colors were Matador Red with a black vinyl top and black interior. Pretty ladies adorned the factory press release photos looking very "mod," "hip," and "with it"—phrases in tune with the times. Although much of the suspension and driveline was basically V-8 Rambler American, the Javelin really was an all-new car.

Many training materials came out in 1968 to inform sales staff of AMC's new corporate attitude change and AMC's serious involvement in racing programs. Headquarters on Plymouth Road knew that when people came into an AMC showroom—many for the first time in their lives—the entire sales and service departments had to be kind, courteous, and knowledgeable about the new AMC cars, especially about the new V-8 engines and the Javelin. Sales training aids such as the "1968 Honest Value Story" were produced. This large brochure was intended to teach salespeople about all the new 1968 AMC cars, but it pushed the Javelin the hardest. The Javelin was the only new model for early 1968, and AMC's image and bank account depended on the car.

The sassy new Javelin could be ordered in the fall of 1967 as a new 1968 model. It came in 14 solid colors outside and black, tan, or red inside. The base Javelin was priced at $2,482.20 plus freight, and came with thin dual pinstripes on the beltline—no rocker panel trim and no hood indentation chrome trim. The seats were all-vinyl, nonreclining buckets in solid black or white Tahiti embossed vinyl basketweave pattern with "antelope" grain vinyl bolsters. There wasn't a woodgrain "V" on the door panels. The base powerplant was a 232-ci inline six, cranking out 145 brake horsepower at 4,300 rpm. For $105, an optional two-barrel 290-ci V-8 with 200 brake horsepower and single exhaust was available. For another $150.35, a four-barrel 290-ci V-8 producing 225 brake horsepower with dual exhaust and chrome tips was fitted to the car. The top engine option was the, 280-horsepower 343-ci V-8 with dual exhaust and chrome tips, which was available in 1968 for $241.05. A two-barrel 343 V-8 wasn't

The Javelin featured a clean, elegant, and refined styling, and along with the AMX, it was AMC bold entry into the musclecar market. It was available with three engines: a base 232-ci six base engine, 290-ci V-8 and a 343-ci V-8.

offered in the Javelin in 1968, though it was an option in the Rebel and Ambassador. This might have been a ploy by AMC marketing to make sure young buyers had as much steam on the strip and street as the 343 could offer. A two-barrel 343 in the new Javelin could get a bad reputation for being a "pooch" and reflect negatively on the new image AMC was attempting to establish.

The mighty AMC 390-ci V-8 was not offered in the Javelin or in any other AMC car in the first part of the year. It came out with major fanfare in the 1968-1/2 AMX in February 1968, halfway through the 1968 production run. When the big "AMX" 390 V-8, pumping out 315 brake horsepower, became available after February 1968 on the Javelin SST, it cost $273.40. But, one had to pop for an "optional" transmission, too—either a Warner Gear Model 12 automatic with floor console ($279.95) or the four-speed manual transmission with no console ($184.25). Although these prices seem dirt-cheap compared to today's prices, one must remember what the average union factory autoworker made in 1968. Average take-home pay for a line worker was $4,500 a year. One hundred dollars was more than a week's gross pay!

Transmissions for the base Javelin were a three-speed, column-shifted manual and a column-shifted, three-speed Warner Gear automatic.

AMC saw sales of the new 1968 Javelin top the 50,000 mark before the end of the model year. Although very good for a pony car two to three years late in the market, Chevrolet sold more than four times as many 1968 Camaro hardtops. Larry Mitchell collection

The 1969 Javelin was little changed from the 1968 model. This example has the AMX 390 V-8 and the rally side stripes: AMC muscle at its best. Larry Mitchell Collection

(AMC bought the automatics from Warner to save costs of making something of its own.) The same transmissions for the 290 V-8 cars, with the addition of the Shift-Command automatic and a console on the floor or a four-speed, could be selected. No consoles were offered with the four-speed cars. All of the above were available on the 343 V-8 Javelins except for the three-speed manual column-shift. All six-cylinder Javelins had a light-duty AMC rear axle assembly, while V-8 cars had the strong AMC Model 20 rear axle with Twin-Grip limited-slip optional. Rear axle ratios for the V-8 cars depended on customer choice and other options selected and included 2.87:1, 3.15:1, and 3.54:1, though the 3.54:1 axle could only be ordered with a four-speed transmission. Factory-optional, dealer-installed engine performance parts and other speed equipment are covered in a sidebar in the AMX chapter.

The "SST" was a deluxe trim package version of the Javelin. The 1968 full-line, color AMC brochure stated that SST stood for either Super Sport Touring, or Super Sonic Transport, or just plain "SST." It was your choice. Again, this shows the humor injected into the sales effort by the Wells, Rich, and Greene advertising agency to break the ice with new customers coming into AMC showrooms. One can't criticize what worked—and it did work.

Remember, the zany TV show *Laugh-In* started in 1969. Fun and comedy were "in." Somewhere along the line, a bull's-eye target emblem complemented the Javelin script, probably intended to soften the impact of the name and reduce any negative connotations.

The SST upgrade on a V-8 Javelin cost $105. For your money you got those famous "Nash heritage" reclining bucket seats in "Ventilair" breathable (knitted) vinyl, nylon reinforced with "antelope"-grain vinyl bolsters in red, tan, or black, or "Strata-Stripe" pattern nylon/viscose fabric with "antelope" grain vinyl bolsters in red, tan, or black. The SST Package also included the deluxe 1967 carry-over imitation woodgrain sports steering wheel with a new center section and interior trim inset on the "V" of the door panels that looks like walnut. Other distinguishing features were SST emblems (and other minor embellishments), stainless-steel rocker panel moldings, SST emblems under the Javelin script on the front fenders, stainless-steel roof gutter trim, and a wide rally stripe, which replaced the twin, thin pinstripes at the upper beltline.

For performance buffs looking to make a muscle-car out of the Javelin, the "Go" Packages were available. For $265.50 on a base Javelin or the SST,

Few ad agencies had the nerve to challenge the American buying public with such an ad inviting people to come in and hammer a new car. AMC had such a negative performance image, they had to be gutsy to get potential buyers into showrooms.

What made the Javelin so unique was the roofline that sloped all the way back to the rear quarter end caps where it gently blended in. No one else did a fastback roof like the Javelin.
Larry Mitchell

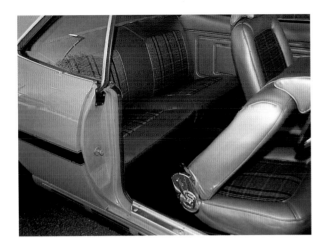

All Javelins had 2+2 seating with buckets in the front and a full back seat. Its two-seat brothers, the 1968, 1969, and 1970 AMX, were a foot shorter behind the front buckets, eliminating the space required for a rear seat. Larry Mitchell

Note the hooded visor over the instrument cluster. This came out as a running change about halfway through 1969. This photo also shows the Hurst shifter and the standard-issue small change tray in lieu of an optional four-speed console. Werner Fruhwirth

the customer received the 280-brake horsepower 343 V-8 with dual exhaust, power front disc brakes (Bendix-brand four-piston calipers with non-vented rotors), E-70 14-inch wide-profile redline tires, handling package (front sway bar, heavy-duty springs and shocks, and 5.5-inch plain steel rims), and wide, side rally stripes. An optional in-dash tachometer replaced the small clock on the far left of the instrument cluster. On non-air-equipped cars, a dealer-installed "Rally Pack" was optional and gave the sports-minded Javelin driver a clock and an over/under Stewart-Warner oil/amp gauge in the center dash panel right above the radio. The overlay had an eyebrow or visor molded in, while the air conditioning overlays were flat. The center dash overlays, except for those of the Rally Pack, were a slight contrast in color to the rest of the dash.

All the typical options on most other manufacturer's cars were optional on the Javelin. These included, but were not limited to the following: air conditioning, power steering and brakes, tilt column, tinted glass, AM or AM/FM radio, AM/8-track stereo tape player with rear speakers, vinyl roof, in-the-dash tachometer, electric wipers, remote outside mirror, and chrome steel "mag" wheels. Lesser items included bulky hubcaps that

imitated a sort of mag wheel so closely that tire shop jockeys were known to twist off the built-in lug nuts before they discovered they were not real mags. Headrests on the back of the seats were an option until they became federally mandated in January 1968.

AMC Launches a Media Blitz

The Wells, Rich, and Greene advertising agency was hired to help turn AMC's stodgy image around. They got right to work and started to take potshots at the Ford Mustang, right to the chin. The first car in the 1968 full-line brochure was the new Javelin with some in-your-face ad copy: "Its price is much less than Mustang's, yet you get more. Javelin is the new-this-year car. (So the '68 will always be the classic.) A Mustang-Camaro-Barracuda class car. But classier. Javelin is the roomiest 4-passenger sports hardtop of them all. With buckets in front and a full back seat. Javelin is larger. Longer. Gives you more leg room front and rear, and a lot more trunk space. Javelin is glassier. Bigger windshield (with rakish slope) and bigger windows everywhere. Like that enormous one-piece side window.

"Wildly more extravagant than the ordinary door-window-vent combination. (And Javelin has flow-through ventilation that works a lot better than vent windows.) Javelin is sleeker. It's made as if the money in it didn't matter." Mary Wells and her team back at the ad agency certainly didn't save any punches in pitching the new Javelin.

Two-page ads appeared in car magazines, as well as in *Look* and *Life* magazines, and featured a red 1967 Mustang with black vinyl top and red interior sitting next to the same color combination of a new 1968 Javelin. The ad copy read like a one-sided boxing match: "Javelin has better styling, more room, larger standard engines and costs less." Other two-page ads pictured a Javelin next to an AMC Rebel sedan. The typical American family consisting of husband, wife, and four kids are standing next to the Rebel, with Dad looking longingly at the new Scarab Gold Javelin. The pitch is the Javelin is what Dad came to look at, but it is not what would be best for the family. He came to look at the Javelin . . . and bought a more practical Rebel sedan. Yet another variation of this ad had a Javelin next to an AMC Rebel with the caption, "Is it stupid to show the Rebel in the same ad with the Javelin?" It goes on, "It takes guts to show the body of our Rebel alongside the racy body of our Javelin. But that's what the Rebel has—guts, the inner guts of a beautiful machine." AMC's bold and brash ad agency even put a Rolls-Royce in a two-page color ad claiming it was unfair to compare a Rolls with

This rare, optional roof spoiler was only available on the Javelins in late 1969 and into 1970. This spoiler was designed for and only fits the roofline of a Javelin, not an AMX. Larry Mitchell

an AMC Ambassador. The Ambassador had more to offer for a lot less money!

Another ad that ran in national car magazines made a direct challenge to the baby-boomer youth market. Bold type in the banner grabbed one by the shirt by saying, "Test Drag a Javelin." The copy then pushes the virtues of the Javelin with a minor slap in the face to the negative attitude the youth market had of AMC. The first line read: "Don't laugh. The Javelin SST is even faster than it looks." The rest of the copy builds up the optional 343 V-8 (the biggest V-8 offered in the first few months of 1968 sales). For the first time ever, a national ad for an AMC car bragged about handling, power, speed, and quarter-mile timeslips. We had come a long way, baby, 15.8 seconds in the quarter-mile! And this came from the mouths of the folks who gave us Ramblers, whose previous ads touted 28 miles per gallon and ease of parking as what we all should dream about in a car.

The "Hey Javelin" campaign had bumper stickers, radio, and local and national TV ads with that catchy dialogue—all to attract attention to the new Javelin. The most famous national TV ad of all featured an average guy in a new Javelin being challenged to drag race away from a stoplight by a guy in an exotic European sports car. The Javelin driver declines the invitation because he has a bowl of goldfish balanced on the passenger seat. Some young girls also challenge the guy and so does a young man on a motorcycle. The Javelin driver declines them all. After all, street racing was going on, but it was not cool to admit it on national TV. The Javelin driver then pulls into a

New for 1969 was a platinum interior, with solid vinyl or cloth inserts. This Javelin has the Hurst four-speed shifter, also new for 1969. Larry Mitchell

The 1969 1/2 Javelin. The looks are both beauty and the beast. This example shows the optional (faux) twin hood scoops and the edge of the roof spoiler peeking over the crest of the roof. Larry Mitchell

parking ramp where the young parking attendant takes his keys. The kid then smokes the tires of the Javelin off-camera, while the Javelin owner just stands there, surprised but understanding.

There was another national TV ad that was cute and attracted a lot of attention. It featured a young man showing his dad his new Javelin parked at the curb in front of the house. When the dad comes down the sidewalk and sees a red Javelin with a blower sticking out of a hole cut in the hood, he comes unglued. The kid comments that he didn't butcher the car, he only made a great car better.

Sweepstakes were a big thing in the 1960s, and AMC's witty advertising agency launched at least three of them in 1968 and 1969. One was the "American Motors FREE-WHEELING Sweepstakes." If your pinwheel entry card matched a certain pattern in the official viewer, you could win a prize. Given away were 1 Ambassador, 2 AMXs, 3 Javelins, 4 Rebels, 5 Americans, 11 motorcycles, 222 bicycles, 333 racers (whatever they were), 444 wagons, 15,555 roller skates, and "umpteen" pinwheels. Note the humor in progressive numbers and the "umpteen" for the number of pinwheels. Other contests were the "His 'N Hers AMX Sweepstakes," in which one could win one of four new AMC cars, including a Javelin. The "Red, White and Blue Sweepstakes" entry form was yet another national contest that drew a lot of participants and new lookers into AMC showrooms.

"Guest drive" was a direct mail campaign with an invitation to come into your local AMC dealer and drive a new 1968 AMC car of your choice. The new Javelin was pictured on the overleaf, but you could choose a cruise in an Ambassador or smoke the tires on a new 390 AMX, if you wanted. You got a free outdoor mural to paste on the den wall just for coming in and letting the sales staff take a whack at you.

To show support for the new AMC Racing Team, you could either go to a local AMC dealer and buy neat racing stuff, or send away to Detroit for the items. All these novelties and premiums sported the new red, white, and blue tricolor racing theme. You could get outside-stick decals for the AMX, Javelin, or Rebel Racing Teams, sew-on patches for hats and jackets, and men's and boys' tri-color nylon windbreakers by Timberline.

AMC contracted with scale model maker Jo-Han to produce 1/25th-scale Javelin promotional models in factory colors. These were to be sold over the parts counter to interested collectors or given away in the showroom to the kids brought in by their parents. The same model cars not

This 1969-1/2 Javelin SST is painted Big Bad Blue and is equipped with the AMX 390, four-speed, "Go" Package, rally wheels, and what is termed the Mod Package, consisting of roof spoiler and simulated side exhaust. Larry Mitchell

painted in authentic colors and with friction/flywheel "motors" were sold on shelves in local model and toy shops, along with glue-together kits of the new Javelin in stock and race form. AMC even had Javelin-logo jewelry made, which included tie tacks and cufflinks and even gold-rimmed glassware. All were offered for sale to AMC dealers to give away or sell. (Scale toys and models of the Javelin were made in the United States and overseas for all the years the Javelin was made, 1968–1974. Javelin toys are still being made today.)

These ads, gimmicks, and promotional items were excellent, as was the whole campaign by Wells, Rich, and Greene. No American carmaker was as bold, as novel, and as humorous as AMC in pitching cars in 1968. It was a major gamble that could have backfired, but it worked and young people, though not in droves, did come into AMC

showrooms and buy cars. After losing $75.8 million in 1967, the ledgers swung into black ink for 1968. The Javelin and the clever ads, sweepstakes, and promotions were a big part of the reason.

Car Magazine Reviews

For its January 1968 issue, *Motor Trend* tested and reported on five cars they categorized as sports-personal cars—Barracuda-340, 4-speed; Camaro-396, 3-speed automatic; Cougar-390, 3-speed manual; Firebird-400, 3-speed manual; Mustang-390, 3-speed manual; and, of course, the Javelin 343, four-speed manual. They printed the following about the Javelin: "American Motors is very sincere in their flattery. They copied the other makers' basic sports-personal idea, but that's where the imitation ends. Their Javelin is a world apart from the other pony cars in styling, comfort, space and features." *Motor Trend*'s report continues, "It

The 1970 Javelin was restyled to suit AMC's marketing department in an attempt to have a bolder look. To accomplish this, the 1970 AMX ram-air hood became an option on any 1970 Javelin with a 360 or 390 four-barrel V-8. The landau-style half-vinyl roof carried over from late 1969. Larry Mitchell collection

also differs in the fact that never has one car meant so much to the corporate life of a company. For AM's sake, Javelin has to be a success. We feel it has to be a success because it is a good product. The car is a good representative for any company's name tag." The Javelin they tested was an early model with the biggest engine offered at that time, the 280-brake horsepower 343 with a four-barrel carburetor and dual exhaust. The Frost White car had the factory T-10 Warner four-speed and a rather tall 3.15:1 ring and pinion.

MT ran the car at Irwindale Raceway through the quarter-mile and said, "Performance of our test car was just short of surprising. Our best elapsed time for the quarter-mile was 15.12 seconds, and this resulted in a speed of 93.26 miles per hour, according to the Chrondeks at Irwindale Raceway."

For comparison's sake, the four other 1968 pony cars were equipped with four-barrel carb V-8s and dual exhaust and rear axle ratios between 3.07 and 3.36. The fastest elapsed time was recorded by the Javelin at 15.1, followed by the Mustang and Barracuda tied at 15.2; Firebird and Cougar tied at 15.4; and Camaro at 15.6. The Barracuda engine was rated at 5 brake horsepower under the 280-brake horsepower Javelin and all the other cars had over 300-brake horsepower engine ratings.

Motor Trend was very impressed with the Javelin's handling dead stock and the ability of the disc/drum setup to stop the car.

MT enjoyed the larger interior space AMC's advertising agency pointed out in the national ads. There was more room everywhere, including in the back seat, than all the other pony cars. One of the things they were not happy about was sthe nonfunctional flow-through ventilation (AMC found this out too—there was very little negative air pressure in the doorjamb to suck out stale air from the cockpit no matter what the ad copy said). In addition, the side windows that were heavy to roll up, and the lock-out ring on the stock four-speed shift lever was less than ideal. But they thought the stock 1968 AMC shifter bought from Ford was one of the better units they had ever tested. *Motor Trend* spoke for most of the other car magazines in really liking the 1968 Javelin, especially when directly compared with the competition. Articles like these in the car buff magazines also helped fill AMC showrooms with interested young buyers—just what AMC needed.

The biggest gripe about the new Javelin was the extensive use of plastic in the interior. The metal dashboards that would crack your jaw like a crab leg were long gone, and all American carmakers had plastic interiors by the late 1960s. Complaints from the buff magazines and Javelin buyers were about the plain, "Spartan" look of the Javelin interior. There was little to break it up or class it up. Those complaints would be addressed and much improved on the 1969 Javelin.

Buyers of Javelins got AMC's new five-year, 50,000-mile warranty. It was a risk AMC took considering a lot of their cars were bound to get flogged hard on the strip and the street.

The optional rally wheels for 1968 were 14x6-inch, all-chrome spyders, and rimmed with satin black indentations and an American Motors–script centercap. Chrysler, Ford, and Chevrolet used similar wheels, but with cosmetic differences. The wheels were made in Detroit by Motor Wheel Corporation for all companies. For those interested in aftermarket wheels for their new Javelin, AMC endorsed Cragar chrome, five-spoke S/S wheels and American Racing Torque Thrust five-spokers. These were factory approved but dealer installed.

When the AMX came out in February 1968, the new "AMX 390" V-8 engine could be ordered in any 1968-1/2 Javelin, Rebel, or Ambassador. The big 390 finally made the Javelin a true, high-performance sports-personal car, especially with a Go Package and a four-speed transmission. Quarter-mile times dipped into the high 14 seconds making the Javelin competitive with most of the other pony cars and quicker than some.

Aftermarket and AMC dealer-installed high-performance parts began to come on line by late 1967. Intake manifolds, cams, headers, carbs, AMX-type traction kits, and more became available from AMC dealers' parts counters or local speed shops. These new AMC high-performance parts are covered in the AMX chapter under Group 19 Parts.

During the first year, 56,462 Javelins were sold. AMC wished for more sales and did everything they could to sell the car. It was hard to change the public's image of an old company known for economy cars and an outspoken antiracing campaign to a new company with a new V-8 engine and serious race cars. Young folks came into AMC dealerships, but in many parts of the country the dealerships were still old fashioned in looks and attitudes. Southern California was a bright spot for Javelin sales in 1968 as were the Upper Midwest and East Coast. Sales in the South were dismal. Still, the Javelin made money for AMC in 1968, and some who came into the world of AMC in 1968 from other American car brands are still here today, and some are leaders of the AMC hobby.

Special-Build Javelins

A special, customized Javelin was done by Puhl's House of Kustoms in Chicago for American Motors to use on the new car introduction show circuit. The car received hidden headlights, a tubular grille treatment, and a hot tangerine paint job with Cragar Super Sport chrome mag wheels. The 1968 Javelin scale-model kit by Jo-Han has the custom parts in the box to build this show car.

A couple of names in customizing and racing were hired to massage the new Javelin and create special customizing kits a new Javelin owner could

bolt on his or her new car. Darel and Larry Droke were Ford racers out of Southern California. They were tapped by the Southern California AMC dealers to put together a package to be sold through AMC dealers nationally or directly from their business, DLR Engineering in Downey. They came up with a fiberglass bolt-on hood that inverted the stock Javelin's twin indentations and made twin scoops out of them. A nice "ducktail" spoiler with end caps was added to the rear trunk lid and Cragar S/S wheels replaced the stock factory wheels. A custom steering wheel, single hoop roll bar, and an "XP" decal rounded out the $550 package. You were supposed to rip out the stock Javelin twin-venturi grille and install a new 1968 AMX grille bought over the counter at the AMC dealer to complete the Droke Brothers XP Package.

Southern Californian "King of the Customizers" George Barris got in on the act under invitation, and for his version of a customized Javelin, he installed a classic tube grille and Shelby Mustang-style fake scoops in front of the rear wheelwell with a painted-on black arrow running forward to the front fender wheelwell. Twin raised scoops sprang up from the fiberglass hood. The factory twin indentations running forward on the hood and the mouth of the front of the car were outlined in satin black paint. The indentation around the rear window was painted satin black and a

The 1970 Javelin Trans-Am Replica. AMC's racing paint scheme was brought to the streets in a true limited-edition of only 100 cars. The T/A Replicas were dead-stock Javelin SSTs with the 390 V-8 and four-speeds. In the days of big-block musclecars of up to 455-ci, they were a tough sell to buyers.

spoiler similar to the XP package was grafted to the trunk. Barris called his creation the Bonanza Package. It was offered through his business or any AMC dealer nationwide.

Few—if any—of these Barris and Droke packages were ever sold. They were a grab for the press and some attention, but too expensive for new car buyers to actually fork out the extra bucks. The rear spoilers were nice on both packages, and the hood treatment on the XP was not unlike what AMC would offer for 1969 on the cars with the factory Go Package. But the majority of new Javelin buyers were back East where cost and conservative attitudes nixed interest in wild ideas coming from Surf City.

The Evolved Second-Year Javelin

The new 1968 Javelin couldn't hold a candle to the sales records set by the 1965 Mustang, but it did well. So American Motors felt the only thing it needed was refinement. Things that were wrong with the car were fixed as "running changes" as the cars came down the line in 1968 and into 1969. This solved some of the customer concerns and new-model engineering glitches.

The 1969 Javelin had the script "Javelin" taken out of the grille and moved to the left leading edge of the hood. A bull's-eye emblem took its place. The grille was slightly changed but kept its twin-venturi look. The Javelin script on the front fenders was moved to the C-pillar now moved up to the exterior sail panels. The new sail panels, and the new, optional rally side stripes were now twin decals, rather than a single stripe running down the entire side of the body. Cars ordered with the performance Go Package now had the dual indentations in the hood filled with non-functional, satin black, plastic fake hood scoops. As cheesy as it sounds, the car looked good with them. A lot of other American cars of the era had hood scoops and geegaws that looked worse, including the Camaro SS.

A number of new colors replaced most of the 1968 colors with red and white remaining carry-overs. Interiors got a lot of new additions. The standard, non-SST interiors were white and charcoal (not black) basket-weave vinyl. The SST Javelins had all-vinyl Ventilair seats in charcoal, platinum, blue, red, and beige, with the same colors being offered as solid vinyl bolsters with "Glengarry" pattern cloth inserts. Interiors on the Javelins could be quite eye-catching to say the least.

Automatic transmission–equipped cars got a new full-length console with a locking glovebox and woodgrain overlays. Matching wood-grain overlays also went on the door armrests and the center dash panel. This touch of simulated wood really spruced up the interior, in answer to complaints about the drabness of the 1968 Javelin interiors.

The standard 3-speed manual transmission was no longer column-shifted, it was floor-shifted. Four-speed cars also lacked a floor console, but did get a new Hurst OEM Competition Plus shifter replacing the (1966–1969-1/2) previous year's unit bought from Ford. This new shifter was a midyear running change.

The base engine in the Javelin was still the 232 six-cylinder, while the 290 two-barrel or four-barrel, 343 four-barrel, and 390 four-barrel were all optional. The Go Package consisted of a 343 or 390 engine with (Carter AFB) four-barrel carb, dual exhausts, power front disc brakes, Polyglas redline tires on 14x6-inch standard steel rims, handling package, and twin (fake) hood scoops. Twin-Grip limited-slip was optional and not a part of the Go Package on the Javelin. The 14x6-inch Styled Steel rally wheels were also optional. For 1969 they were now "Charcoal-Glitter" spyders, satin black indentations with a brushed-look, stainless-steel snap-on trim ring, and an AMC center cap. A full-sized, in-dash tachometer now sat next to the matching 140-miles-per-hour speedometer, optional as one unit. All the other 1968 options carried over into 1969 including a rarely ordered option, air conditioning. A new interior addition was a center bolster bolted to the floor between the seats with a drop-down, padded armrest for the manual-shift cars.

In 1969-1/2, AMC decided to get with the psychedelic times by offering new colors on its performance cars as Chrysler had done. A special brochure announcing "Who's afraid of the Big Bad Colors?" heralded the arrival at your local AMC dealer of Javelins (and AMXs) in Big Bad Blue, Big Bad Orange, and Big Bad Green. These colors were neon bright and were hinting strongly of the drug culture of the time. AMC said in the brochure, ". . . they're the boldest street machine skin covers since candy apple anythings and red lead primer." The brochure even had wavy images as if these cars were floating through space—and your mind. Cheech and Chong might have loved the Big Bad Javelins if they weren't into smoke-filled, 1964 Chevy lowriders.

You could get the Big Bad Colors on any Javelin, including a base 232 six-cylinder model, though most folks ordered an optional V-8 and the SST upgrade package. Optional on the Big Bad–painted Javelins were a revised and repositioned version of the 1968 Breedlove Javelin Speed

A 1970 Mark Donohue Special Javelin SST. This car is one of 2,501 produced to homologate the Javelin for SCCA Trans-Am racing. It is optioned with the 390 engine and a four-speed and the man who ordered it new still owns it today. Larry Mitchell

Spectacular roof spoiler (never available on an AMX as the roofline is different); a new reverse "C" stripe in red, white, or black running down the sides of the car; and simulated side exhaust rocker panels. If you ordered the Go Package with the corresponding engine, you got the twin, satin black, fake hood scoops. All Big Bad cars had bumpers devoid of normal chrome and were painted matching body color. The 1969-1/2 "mod-pack" Javelin SST with the roof spoiler, hood scoops, simulated side exhaust, reverse "C" stripe, styled steel rally wheels, and redlines was simply gorgeous to behold, and with a 390 under the hood it was automotive cheesecake. Sexy with a capital "S." Like wow, man.

Foreign Javelins

In 1969, AMC sent approximately 200 knocked-down Javelin SSTs to Germany. Karmann, the maker of the Karmann Volkswagens, assembled the cars, trimmed them out, and sold them in Europe. The cars were badged on the rear

The rear ducktail spoiler with Donohue's replica signature identifies the Mark Donohue Special 1970 Javelin. This car has the optional 15-inch "Rebel Machine" rally wheels. Larry Mitchell

quarter near the side window, "Javelin 79-K." The "79" was AMC's model designation and the "K" was for Karmann. All were 343 V-8 cars with automatic transmission. Few are accounted for today, and none are known to be in the United States.

About 200 knocked-down 1969 Javelin SSTs fitted with 343 V-8s and automatics were sold to Australian Motor Industries in Melbourne, which assembled them with a custom dash as right-hand-drive vehicles. One associated chapter of AMC World Clubs, the Javelin Registry in Melbourne, tries to keep track of these cars in Australia. They are the Javelin Registry in Melbourne. Select-year Javelins were assembled in Australia until 1974.

Starting in 1969, American Motors dealers got quantities of a new two-color newsletter from AMC that exclusively covered AMC's racing efforts. It was available to the general public at AMC

dealer showrooms every couple of months. This publication *The Redliner*, was published until 1972.

AMC Revamps the 1970 Javelin

AMC executives were scratching their collective heads over why sales of the Javelin went down for 1969. They felt a restyle was in order, so new interiors and some sheet-metal changes were on the menu for the 1970 version, including a slightly longer nose and a subtly revised grille and front bumper. The new ram-air hood to be standard on the 1970 AMX became optional on the 1970 Javelins with a four-barrel V-8. The standard hood looked similar to the 1969 Go Package hood treatment, but with fake chrome intakes.

The taillights changed a little although the rear bumper remained the same, and the vinyl roof option covered only half the roof and provided a landau look. Inside, the 1970 Javelin got a completely new dash with a large, flat, silver-gray overlay and matching glovebox door for the base Javelin; a woodgrain overlay was used for the SST. The floor console had matching woodgrain overlays around the shifter and the new, lockable glovebox door on any Javelins ordered with the automatic on the floor. New seats were standard, high back, and nonreclining.

Door panels changed, as did seat materials, which could be ordered in standard Ventilair breathable solid vinyl or the new, optional "Corduroy" solid ribbed cloth in black, light blue, medium green, bright red, or medium saddle tan. Leather was also a new Javelin option for the seats in red, black, or saddle tan. A new "rim-blo" horn steering wheel was available in the 1970 Javelin, similar to those in some Ford and Mercury cars of the same year.

Fourteen exterior colors were available, with white and red being carry-overs for the third year. The Big Bad Colors were available on the new Javelins, with chrome bumpers. The optional side strip was a reverse "C" with the top portion running the entire length of the body. The optional, dealer-installed deck-lid luggage rack of previous year's car was now factory installed.

The Go Package for 1970 consisted of a 360 or 390 four-barrel motor, AMX ram-air hood with functional intakes, dual exhaust, power front disc brakes, E70x14 Polyglas redline tires (changed to small, raised white letter tires early into the year), 6-inch regular rims with hubcaps, and the Handling Package.

Without the Go Package, the ram-air hood was nonfunctional. Rally wheels were the carry-over 1969 units, but the SST cars could have a 15x7 argent silver-colored rally wheel with an AMC chrome center that was standard on the 1970 Rebel Machine.

Variable-ratio power steering replaced the fixed ratio on the 1968–69 cars, and a locking steering column with built-in key ignition (GM Saginaw) became standard. The standard engine was the 145-brake horsepower 232 six-cylinder. Optional engines were the 210-brake horsepower 304 two-barrel V-8, a 245-brake horsepower 360 two-barrel V-8, a 290-brake horsepower 360 four-barrel V-8, and a 325-brake horsepower 390 four-barrel V-8. The transmissions were a three-speed manual floor-shift, which was standard on the six, while a column-shifted automatic was optional. The 304 V-8 got the three-speed manual setup, the column automatic, or a floor-shift automatic with full-length console. The 360

two-barrel motor had a column- or floor-shifted automatic, both at extra cost. The 360 four-barrel engine had the column or floor automatic with the Warner Gear T-10 four-speed manual with Hurst shifter, all optional. The 390 V-8 (only sold as a four-barrel engine) had a floor-shift, full console automatic or the four-speed, both at additional cost. V-8 production rear axle gears were available with 2.87:1, 3.15:1, or 3.54:1 gearing, depending on the engine and transmission ordered.

The big news for the 1970 engines was the "D-port" or "dogleg" head design that AMC Engineering and Dave Potter had discovered when bench flowing the 1969 heads for Kaplan Engineering on the Trans-Am Javelins. They found that if the shape of the exhaust port on the heads were "L" shaped rather than square shaped, the heads would flow nearly 50 percent more volume under full race conditions. This new head design was put into production for 1970 on all the AMC V-8s: 304, 360, and 401. New exhaust manifolds for the 1970 series of V-8s had the dogleg design, but retained their log-style shape.

Shortly into the 1970 run of production car engines, the cam specs changed and a new cam known as the "white stripe" cam was installed in all engines. Although advertised horsepower figures did not go up much, performance did increase for the 1970 V-8 cars. The insurance industry was cracking down on musclecars by 1970 due to large claim losses caused by young drivers wrapping the factory hot rods around telephone poles. If a musclecar hit the magic 10-pounds-of-weight-per-one-(engine) horsepower ratio, the owner got nailed with a major premium surcharge.

A second bit of big news for 1970 was the new, double balljoint front suspension replacing the (Deep Coil Ride) trunnion system. The 1970 Javelin rode smoother and softer than the 1968 and 1969 models, and some say the handling was also improved.

Special Javelins

AMC had made enough changes on the suspension, body, and engines for 1970 that the car had to be homologated all over again in order to be legal to race in the 1970 Trans-Am series. This meant that American Motors had to make a minimum of 100 identical street cars to legalize the basic body, suspension, and driveline for racing. Ford built the Boss 302s and Chevrolet built the Camaro Z-28s to meet the homologation rules.

In the fall of 1969, AMC made 100 identical 1970 Javelin SSTs, all painted in the hash red, white, and blue scheme similar to the real 1968–69 Trans-Am Javelin race cars. Nothing quite so knock-your-socks-off bold had ever been sold to the general public by an American car-maker before, and it is suspected that the tri-color paint scheme on these cars was the idea of AMC's outlandish ad agency. The similarities were more than just paint deep. The cars were all optioned the same with the big 390 engine, four-speeds with the factory Hurst shifter, 3.91.1 rear gears with Twin-Grip limited-slip, functional AMX ram-air blister hood, Go Package, power steering, front disc brakes, heavy-duty handling and cooling, factory rally wheels with Goodyear Polyglas SRWL tires, AM radio, tachometer, and other lesser amenities. To complete the racing look—as if the "cop-bait" paint job wasn't enough—the stand-up rear wing spoiler of the real 1968–69 Trans-Am Javelin race car was bolted to the trunk lid and a front, full-length fiberglass spoiler was screwed to the fenders be-low the front bumper. (It has been reported that each of the 100 cars came with the front spoiler, but this author saw some new ones that did not have the front spoiler.)

The 100 Trans-Am Javelin Street Replicas were advertised in various national magazines with an authentic 1969 race car (and driver) next to the Replica with an snooty, mousy-looking guy lean-ing on the fender with a scarf around his neck and a smirk on his face.

Wells, Rich, and Greene may have gone over-board with trying to be cute with this ad, for few buyers got turned on identifying with the wimp leaning on the street version. These cars are very collectible today, but were hard sells on the showroom floors in the fall of 1969. Some poten-tial buyers were at first attracted to the paint job, then, when reality set in, they rejected it—and the car itself.

Buyers knew the loud, hash colors would at-tract the fuzz. The paint would also attract street racers who lurked around virtually every intersec-tion in every town in America in 1970. With only 325 horsies under the hood, the owner of a Trans-Am Javelin Replica had to stay away from 455 H.O. Oldsmobiles, 454 Chevelles, 427 Corvettes, and a host of other big-block factory musclecars. With no rear sway bar (actually a bigger front with a rear bar as a package), the car was also not up to snuff with the Z-28s, Boss Mustangs, 442s, and other 1970 musclecars that would outhandle the Javelin on a slalom course.

One buyer in Rockford, Illinois, had his 1970 Trans-Am Javelin Replica repainted from the hash to a solid color by 1972, which was a typical fate of

T/A Javelins and is probably why so few of the 100 original cars survived. Such a fate was unfortunate, because these cars are historic and serious atten-tion-grabbers at shows today.

After all the efforts AMC went through to pro-duce and sell the 100 Trans-Am Replica 1970 Javelins, the SCCA changed its rules. By January 1970 and just months before the season's open-ing race, they increased the required number of street cars to 2,500 in order to homologate the ba-sic car for Trans-Am racing at sanctioned tracks for the summer of 1970. So, AMC had to start all over again.

This time, learning from poor sales of the brash red, white, and blue Replicas, AMC de-cided to use Mark Donohue's name on a version of the 1970 Javelin that could be ordered in any of the normal Javelin production-line colors. Selling 2,500 units was much more likely to hap-pen if the customers could pick their own exte-rior and interior colors. Donohue was on the payroll, having been hired with Roger Penske to field the 1970 Javelin Trans-Am race cars. And Donohue had a hand in choosing the rear duck-tail spoiler used in racing and on the street cars. Why not use his name to help sell the 1970 "Donohue" Javelins?

AMC featured national ads showing the 1970 Donohue Javelin in Big Bad Orange, a popular color. Customers ordering the car could have any other standard 1970 color they wanted, inside or out. AMC (R. W. McNealy) finally got around to homologating a much-needed engine block with four-bolt main provisions like Kaplan had wanted and had hand-built in the winter of 1968. The rear ducktail spoiler with the Mark Donohue signature decal and the special 360-ci block (standard for this model) were the only unique characteristics of the 1970 Mark Dono-hue Special Javelins. But for some unknown rea-son, many of the Donohue Javelins got standard, production-line 390 engines. The cars were all supposed to be SSTs, but some were not. A buyer could have a four-speed or an automatic with floor-shift and console, but some cars were col-umn-shifted and lacked a console. All were sup-posed to have functional ram air, but some had nonfunctional hoods. Ditto on Go Packages, too. Other than that, a buyer could order what other options he or she wanted, including air condi-tioning, which very few customers did.

All the Donohue cars came with rally wheels, Polyglas tires, and that beautiful rear deck spoiler Donohue robbed off his 1969 Camaro race car. A total of 2,501 Mark Donohue Javelins were sold. Interestingly, Donohue bought one and gave it to

The 1970 AMX ram-air hood was an option on any 360 or 390 four-barrel Javelin for 1970. The twin inlets matched the twin-venturi of the Javelin grille giving a smooth, balanced look to the front end of the car. Larry Mitchell

his mother to drive. Many owners fitted standard Javelins with the special Donohue parts. Thus, there are Donohue Javelins out there that AMC never built. The problem is that AMC did not identify these 2,501 cars as being Donohue Javelins in the VIN or anywhere else on the cars. Hence, without an original invoice, bill of sale, or window sticker, there is no positive way to document a Mark Donohue Javelin as being real . . . or not.

Car Magazine Reviews

Only three national magazines road-tested a 1970 390-powered Javelin, and none got the car to run less than 15 seconds in the quarter-mile; the best time was 15.11 by the testers at *Car Life* (December 1969). With improvements in the heads, a new Motorcraft four-barrel carb, and the white-stripe cam, what gives?

The answer is that most auto manufacturers—except AMC—prepped their musclecars and even outright cheated before they gave their "production line" cars to the national magazines to test and get drag results.

Young buyers bought hot factory cars based on buff magazines' published quarter-mile times. Detroit knew this and some cars even had undisclosed blueprinted engines. AMC, good or bad, never did this.Their quarter-mile times were not always up with the Big Three cars, but they were

honest. In the same issue of *Car Life*, a 1970 Dodge Challenger powered by a Six-Pack (three two-barrels) 440 V-8 bolted to a four-speed with a 3.55.1 Sure-Grip differential only managed a 14.64—only a half-second faster than the 390 Javelin, with 65 more horsepower. It's a good guess that the Challenger was a dead-stock car like it should have been.

Negatively affecting the performance of the 1970 Javelin were the puny little E70 Polyglas tires that could be smoked like an Alaskan salmon (a problem with most of the other Detroit muscle-cars, too). Performance killers on the 1970 360 and 390 motors were a lean Motorcraft four-barrel (emissions) and the factory stock cigar-shaped exhaust manifolds, both restricting airflow in and out of the engines. A set of headers and a Holley carb woke up these engines and regularly produced high-13-second quarter-mile times.

Generally, the buyers loved the look of the 1970 Javelins, especially in full dress with the AMX ram-air hood. The national car magazines also liked the 1970 Javelin. In Matador Red with a white vinyl landau roof, white "C" stripe, red leather interior, ram-air hood with a 390 under it, and rally wheels, the 1970 Javelin could just take your breath away. Total Javelin sales for 1970 dropped to 28,210—a disappointment for such a handsome pony car.

four

Javelin 1971–1974
The Bold Restyle

At 19,134 units, sales of the two-seater AMX were not what AMC had hoped for, and everyone at AMC knew it. Dick Teague, being a sports car aficionado, desperately wanted the car to continue into 1971 as a two-seater. He had ideas in the back corners of the Advanced Styling Studios on Plymouth Road.

He sent this author a letter and two personal photographs with the following letter dated June 4, 1984: "The [two] snaps were styling proposals of a possible heavy facelift of the 1970 two-passenger to suggest a 1971 continuation of the two-passenger concept. The investment required to do this was considered much too high for quarters, roof, decklid, backlight, hood, grille, etc. The blue snap is a production model, of course." The snapshot shows a car with humped fenders in the front and what could be a throwback to the fins on the rear of many cars in the late 1950s. The car appears to be a pushmobile and the setting is the Styling Studios on Plymouth Road.

Teague said AMC bought a new 1968 Corvette, and the car was driven into the Advanced Styling Studios as soon as they got it from a local dealer in Detroit. He even admitted they were looking for lines and shapes they could use in restyling either the 1970 AMX or the Javelin for 1971, and the humped fender idea that wound up on the mock-up in the snapshot came directly from the Corvette. The proposal of a major restyling of the 1970 two-seater AMX to be a 1971 model died due to production costs and projected low sales numbers.

Teague's last-ditch effort was to bring his 1969 AMX company car in to the Styling Studios and see what he could do to make a 1971 two-seater proposal cheaper. It is not known if the fiberglass front end came off the finned quarter panel mock-up or not, but as an AMC historian, I'd put money

This 1972 black Javelin SST is a rare 401 V-8 car with the Pierre Cardin designer interior. It also has the rare factory-approved, dealer-installed TADCO Trendsetter sidepipes and "Machine" 15-inch wheels. Bruce Jacobsen

This is a rare, private photograph of what Dick Teague proposed as the 1971 two-seat AMX. The photograph is dated September 26, 1969. Note the pseudo-1950s fins. Many styling characteristics were incorporated into the 1971 Javelin. Larry Mitchell collection

on the chance they did. The humped fender front end wound up on his company driver with the rest of the exterior left as plain 1968–69. Teague snatched the new interior from the Interior Department of the Styling Studios, the next door down the hallway. The red corduroy highback seats and door panels that were 1969 ideas became 1970 Javelin production realities.

These went in the car and it was repainted on the outside from white to a light-blue metallic. The 1968 AMX with the red 1970 corduroy interior and the fiberglass humped fender front end was then presented to the upper brass as the last-gasp effort to continue the production of the 1970 two-seater AMX into 1971 for a lot less money.

This is a factory photo of a second proposal of a 1971 two-seater dated November 4, 1969. This version uses a dead-stock 1968 rear quarter panel instead of the finned effect. It is possible this car and the one in the photo are the same car. It is known that this car was Dick's 1968 production AMX company driver turned into a styling exercise. This front end was used on the 1971 Javelin. Larry Mitchell collection

The Javelin was restyled for 1971 and, especially with the AMX Package and a 401, had the looks of a race car on the streets. This preproduction car had a droop-nose hood stripe that was changed before the actual production run started. Larry Mitchell collection

This 1973 black Javelin AMX has the optional Cardin multicolored interior. This Javelin has the 360 four-barrel engine with the Go Package. Note the Cardin emblem on the front fender. Bruce Jacobsen

The French designer Pierre Cardin signature interior was basic black cloth with swirls of white, silver plum, and Chinese Red along the seats, headliner, and door panels. Javelins with this option are highly collectible, especially as an AMX. Jeff Sorenson

The 1973 AMC low-compression 360, four-barrel V-8 was still powerful enough to obtain quarter-mile time slips in the low 15-second range in dead-stock trim. This engine gets a boost in performance from the optional cowl-induction hood system seen on the top of the air breather. Jeff Sorenson

Teague told me that R. W. McNealy came into his office one day, right after the in-house showing of the 1968/71 car, sat down, and asked Teague his personal thoughts about making the two-seater into 1971. Teague said he was all for it, which was why he was trying to cut costs by using his personal AMX for corporate show-and-tell. Teague said McNealy lamented the fact that the break-even on the two-seater—the way they were making it, out of the Javelin—was 10,000 units a year. Sales in 1968 and 1969 didn't make break-even and they were into the 1970 production run. Sales of the restyled 1970 AMX were dismal at best—about 100 cars a week at the Kenosha plant. McNealy told Teague he and the upper management were going to have to nix the two-seater after the end of production in July 1970.

The 1971 Production Car

Javelin sales were also far below what AMC had hoped for, but it was to continue into 1971 as a cosmetically restyled car. It is rumored that Mark Donohue saw Teague's hump-fendered 1968/71 car and loved the front end, and reportedly said the humps on the fenders, with the matching humps on the rear quarters, would allow for serious racing rubber on the 1971 Trans-Am Javelins. Whatever the truth is, it came to pass that the restyled 1971 Javelin had the humps and became one of most unique-looking, personal-sports cars to ever come out of Detroit. The company battle cry on the front of the 1971 full-line catalog was, "If you had to compete with GM, Ford and Chrysler what would you do?" Collectors today lovingly call the 1971–74 cars the hump-fendered Javelins.

The 1971 Javelin hit showrooms in the fall of 1970, and like many other pony cars, it grew in wheelbase, length, width, and weight. Three levels of trim were offered: a base model, the more deluxe SST, and the top-of-the-line Javelin AMX. Teague said he wasn't in favor of using the AMX name on a four-passenger Javelin, but those above him were. It was the marketing department's idea. And so the AMX name pioneered on the 1968–1970 two-seater became a specially trimmed version of the four-seater 1971 Javelin SST.

The base Javelin came with a 232 six-cylinder, but a new 258 six-cylinder was optional. Also up the engine option ladder were a 304 two-barrel, a 360 with either a two- or four-barrel, and the new 401 V-8 at the top rung. The new 401 was simply the old 390 with a slight increase in stroke for emission purposes. Teague also said the increase to 401 was needed by marketing to try to boost the image of the engine since so many Detroit V-8 musclecars had engines over 400 ci.

The only major external differences between the 1971–72 and the 1973–74 Javelins were in the grilles and the taillights. The 1971 taillight style can be seen on the left, while the 1973–74 style is on the right. Adam Ortiz

Transmissions ranged from a column-shifted, three-speed manual (only on the 232 I-6), to a three-speed manual on the floor or automatic on the floor for the 258-six; a three-speed manual on the floor, automatic on the column or on the floor for the two- or four-barrel 360 V-8s; and an automatic on the floor or column for the 401-equipped cars. A four-speed manual transmission with floor shift was available on the 360 four-barrel or 401 (mandatory four-barrel) V-8s.

Although compression ratios dropped on the V-8s from as much as 10.2:1 in 1969 down to 9.5:1 on the early 1971 401—and even lower on the 401 a few months into production—the brake horsepower figures remained about the same as 1970 on the 360 engines, and went up to 330 brake horsepower on the 401. A reason for this could have been the new "free-flow" cast-iron exhaust manifolds. Unlike previous years' cigar-shaped manifolds, these units were asymmetrical and swooped down to meet the headpipe. AMC's performance guideline booklet, *Performance American Style,* published a year later, stated these new exhaust manifolds flowed "almost as well as headers." That may have been an overstatement, but they did give the V-8s a noticeable kick in the slats. They were standard, and were identical on all 304, 360, and 401 engines from 1971 up.

AMC canned the two-seater as a separate car, but put all the money saved into a completely new

skin for the 1971 Javelin. It looked like a Javelin, but certainly not like anything else on the road. The look was very different compared to the 1970 version. The grille was new, but still kept the twin-venturi look; the hood had a "T" sculpted into it that also ran over the center of the roof creating a "T-top" removable panel look, especially when the vinyl top option was installed. The taillights were different, but the rear bumper remained the same as the 1968–70 unit. The front bumper had to be one of the thinnest and weakest unit ever installed on an American car. But the "pencil-thin mustache" bumper did complement the looks of the front end.

Inside, the interior retained the nonreclining, high-back bucket seats of the 1970 Javelin, but a completely new console and "stirrup-grip" shifter lever were on the floor between the seats of the cars ordered with a floor-shifted automatic. For the first time, a full-length floor console was available as an option for a floor-shift, four-speed. The Hurst shifter continued, and door panels changed from vinyl coverings to a solid sheet of formed plastic.

The big news was the dash, which took on a dramatic new look one either loved or hated. The instrument cluster was curved in front of the driver and everything was easy to read. What some buyers didn't like was the lack of a dash in front of the passenger. Although it was roomy in front of the rider, it did give some an insecure feeling that

The final year of the Javelin was 1974. This Plum metallic 1974 Javelin AMX is a fine example of the last hurrah for American Motors' pony car, the Javelin. Jerry Heasley

there wasn't much between him or her and the windshield. Base and SST Javelins had plastic woodgrain overlays. There are those who love the general interior of the 1971 Javelin and others who have never quite warmed up to it.

Standard vinyl was Tampico-embossed with grained-vinyl bolsters in four colors. Optional was Wellington pleated vinyl in black, blue, green, or red. By October 1970 white was available. Corduroy continued from 1970 in the same colors, except for white. Finally, black or red leather was now available.

There were 14 exterior colors with a simple, single beltline stripe on the base and twin rally stripes at the beltline for the SST in white or

black. The 14x6-inch steel rally wheels carried over from 1970, as did the steel Rebel Machine 15x7-inchers, both using Polyglas-belted SRWL tires. A new wheel was a silver-painted, steel 14x6-inch slotted-type.

The AMX package on the Javelin made one of the meanest-looking street cars ever to come from an American car manufacturer. In the proper colors and options, the 1971 Javelin AMX would just knock your socks off with smooth and graceful, yet powerful lines. Look up the word "macho" in the automotive dictionary and you will find a picture of a 1971 Javelin AMX. You would be hard pressed to recall an American car that looked more like a serious race car wearing street rubber.

It has been rumored for years that Mark Donohue had a hand in suggesting exterior trim for the Javelin AMX he would race on the track in 1971. The ducktail spoiler was right off his 1970 Donohue Special Javelins, and some say that he dictated the look of the front spoiler, which was different from any previous 1970 spoiler optional on the Trans-Am Replica Javelin. The reverse cowl-induction, raised Javelin AMX hood is not unlike the 1969 Z-28. A nice touch credited to Donohue was the wire mesh screen in front of the deeply recessed 1971 grille, but the 1969 Dodge Charger 500 might have had that look first. The hood stripe was, at first, to be drooped over the nose, 1967 Camaro-style, but someone got cold feet and changed it to a flared "T" with tips running back along the tops of the fenders as the production for 1971 started. Inside, the dash overlays and door panels featured aluminum engine-turned trim, a classic beauty.

The Madison Avenue ad agency of Wells, Rich, and Greene said it all in an ad that read, "We made the Javelin the hairiest looking sports car in America, even at the risk of scaring some people off. We may lose a few librarians for customers, but we think we'll gain a few enthusiasts." That statement honked off some librarians, but no enthusiast groups complained.

All the options one could have gotten the years before were available on the new 1971 Javelins. It should be noted that throughout all the years the Javelin was produced, it was never available with cruise control, power windows, power locks, or power seats.

The AMX Package consisted of a base 360 two-barrel V-8 with single exhaust, a three-speed manual, floor-shifted transmission with console, no armrest, nonfunctional cowl hood, silver 8-slot, 14-inch or charcoal 5-spoke rally wheels with 70-series Goodyear tires, rear (only) spoiler, mesh grille screen, clock, and AMX badges. The Go Package on the Javelin AMX was a 360 four-barrel or 401 four-barrel V-8, dual exhaust, cowl-air carburetion (functional hood intake), hood T-stripe, black rear panel, 15x7-inch slot-style wheels (Machine wheels), E60x15 Polyglas white-lettered tires, Space-Saver spare tire, handling package, Twin-Grip differential, power disc brakes, Rally-Pac instruments (includes in-dash Tic-Tac clock/tachometer), and heavy-duty engine cooling (seven-blade fan and shroud).

Car Magazine Reviews

Generally, the automotive press liked the revised Javelin. They liked the looks, ride, and comfort of the car. The new 401 was still the old 390 in

most every way except that it had a smidgen more of stroke, but oh, would it run with those new free-flowing factory exhaust manifolds! The 1971 Javelin was heavier than ever before, which is almost always a killer of quarter-mile times. Other American musclecars that ran in the 14s in 1970 were now turning in the 15s with their lower compression and smog controls. But the AMC 401 motors in any AMC car were still very quick. *Super Stock and Drag Illustrated* hammered a loaded (including air conditioning) 401, four-speed Javelin AMX with optional 3.91:1 Twin-Grip; right off the showroom floor and through the mufflers, *SS/DI* got a best run of a 14.30-second elapsed time at nearly 100 miles per hour.

The magazine also tested a 1971 Boss 351 Mustang that ran a best of 13.93 seconds and a 1971 Ford Torino 429 CJ-R that ran a best of a 14.49-second elapsed time in the quarter. *Supercar '71* magazine drag-tested a 1971 Javelin with the 401 (Borg-Warner) automatic with 3.54:1 gears out back and ripped off a 14.55-second quarter-mile at a tick under 98 miles per hour. When the other musclecars started to suffer performance losses due to desmogged motors, the AMC V-8s came alive—even though the 1971 Javelin AMX with all the toys tipped the scales at close to 3,600 pounds! A lot of that was due to AMC's serious racing efforts and applying what they learned at the street level. Unfortunately, the AMC cars took a major hit in the quality control department due to poor assembly.

As many raves as the 1971 Javelin got for looks and performance, only 28,866 were sold; of that number 2,054 were Javelin AMXs.

The 1972–1974 Javelins

Although AMC sales were up slightly over previous years, money was tight by 1972, and Javelin sales weren't improving the situation. The peak of the factory hot rods was in 1970, and smog regulations were strangling the performance capabilities of the American musclecars that ran carburetors. Even the sales of pony cars were on the decline, with a few exceptions. The Javelin continued production, but only minor cosmetic changes of colors, interior materials, and exterior trim made a 1972 model different from a 1973 or a 1974. A new, silver-painted, 15x7-inch slotted, steel rally wheel replaced the Rebel Machine wheels.

Highlights between the years were also noteworthy. AMC got into designer packages for some of its cars during this time and the Javelin got a famous-name designer touch. An option on the 1972 and 1973 Javelin SSTs in certain exterior colors was the Pierre Cardin interior. The famous

The unique dash of the 1971–74 Javelin AMX had a classic engine-turned overlay with the controls in a semicircle around the driver. This photo shows the optional Rally Instrument Package with the "Tic-Tac" clock/tachometer. Jerry Heasley

French designer really jazzed up the interior on the Cardin Javelins with some of the wildest fabrics and patterns ever seen in any American car. The basic black cloth front and back seats got a rush of contrasting color with Chinese red, plum, white, and silver cloth running across the seat bottoms, backs, door panels, and headliner. Cardin badges adorned the interior door panels and graced the front fenders. Beautiful as it was, it was too loud for some buyers, but today, the 4,152 Cardin Javelins built in 1972 and 1973 are highly prized by AMC collectors.

American carmakers, under governmental and insurance industry pressure, revised how engine horsepower figures were determined for their engines in 1972. The old "gross" power figures were arrived at with the engine on a test stand with no accessories, nearly open exhaust, and no driveline friction losses. Measured this way, the early 1971 401 V-8 produced 330-brake horsepower. The SAE's new "net" figures more accurately represented the engine's output as installed in the vehicle's engine bay, with average accessories and belts hooked up, suffering normal friction driveline losses and as measured at the rear wheels. Measured this way, the 1972 401 V-8 had 255 net horsepower. The 1972 401 got a drop in compression down to 8.5:1 to use regular-grade gasoline, but if one were to measure the brake horsepower for comparison to a 1971 401, the 1972 version would have about 300 brake horsepower.

A major downer for 1972 was the substitution of the 304 two-barrel, single-exhaust V-8 as the base motor in the Javelin AMX over the 360 two-barrel, single-exhaust motor.

The good news for 1972 was the abandonment of the antiquated Warner Gear (Borg-Warner) automatic transmissions in favor of units built for AMC by Chrysler. These were based on the more modern and user-friendly Chrysler Models 904, 998, and the rugged, older 727. The AMC Torque Command 727 came from the Chrysler Torque-Flite 727 automatics used behind engines as mighty as the 426 Hemi and 440 Six-Pak cars. (However, the Chrysler and AMC versions do not directly interchange.) For those who wanted a performance AMC car with an automatic transmission, the new Chrysler-based Torque Command was a blessing. It could even be highly modified for serious performance and control—something the Warner unit could not offer.

A total of 26,184 Javelins were made in 1972; 2,729 as AMX models. The 1973–74 Javelins got new, large, square taillights and the imitation T-top roof lines were eliminated in favor of a flat roof. Large rubber bumperettes were bolted onto the front and rear bumpers to meet new standards, and the V-8 engine got an EGR (exhaust gas recirculation) valve. Catalytic converters were never required on V-8 Javelins, but engine performance suffered somewhat in 1973 and 1974 nonetheless. The Cardin interior continued to be an option on select colors of the 1973 Javelin and Javelin AMX.

Javelin production for 1973 totaled 30,902 cars, including 5,707 AMX models. Javelin production for 1974—its last year—was 27,536, and 4,980 units of that total were AMXs.

Car Magazine Reviews

Road Test magazine took a 1973 401 four-speed Javelin with the 3.91:1 rear Twin-Grip and still did the quarter-mile in a respectable 15.4 seconds at 91 miles per hour. By 1974 compression was lowered in the 360 and 401 V-8s down from 8.50:1 to 8.25:1—nearly a full two points lower than the 1969 390—and performance suffered as smog-related limitations took their toll. The day of the American musclecar was coming to an end, and it would be all but forgotten until electronic fuel injection brought it back a decade later.

Special Javelins

Many state highway patrol agencies use high-performance Mustangs and Camaros for high-speed pursuit purposes. The Alabama Highway Patrol was having problems with speeders on certain interstate roads until the department bought 100

The rear spoiler of the 1971-74 Javelin AMXs was slightly different from the earlier 1970 Donohue version. The rear deck-lid spoilers have to be the most attractive of any musclecar. Jerry Heasley

Javelins equipped with the 401 V-8, automatic transmission and 3.54:1 rear axle. The cars were painted light blue metallic with a dark blue hood and had the 15-inch AMX rally wheels, AMX rear spoiler, no back seat (on some), a Motorola VHF police radio on the console, a single blue light on the roof, "State Trooper" decal on the rear spoiler, and full state decals in blue on the doors.

Somebody at AMC decided to try and celebrate the two back-to-back Trans-Am wins with the Javelin by offering a special package on any 1973 Javelin with a V-8 engine. It was called the Trans-Am Victory Package and consisted of E70-14 Poly-glas RWL tires on 14x6-inch slot-style rally wheels, a Space Saver spare tire, and a nifty decal stating the Javelin was the Trans-Am winner in 1971 and 1972. A decal went on the lower portion of the front fender, just ahead of the door opening. The package listed for $167.45. Nothing identified the car as such in the VIN or trim tags—it was just a stick-on decal that was also available at the AMC parts counters for a few bucks. It was a nice thought, though.

This bumper sticker was free to anyone who came into an American Motors dealer in 1971. It was AMC's moment in the sun and the biggest national racing event they ever won. The same sticker was available in 1972 when they won the 1972 Trans-Am, but it said "Trans-Am Winner, 1971 and '72." Larry Mitchell

five

AMX 1968-1970
From Dream Car to Production Car

AMC toyed with the idea of a two-seat sports car as part of the Project IV show cars. The fully functional, hand-built car known as the Vignale AMX cost AMC a pretty penny to create. In 1966, AMC lost $12.6 million and suffered a 12 percent sales decline, causing AMC management to think twice about what new cars were needed in the dealers' showrooms and how much they were going to cost to produce. By 1966, the emerging youth musclecar market was established and accounted for the lion's share of overall sales. A pony car was a big part of what AMC needed—and it needed it as soon as possible.

The Ambassador was new for 1967, as was the Rebel, which shared the same basic unibody and much of the external sheet metal and trim with the Ambassador. The Javelin was given the go-ahead by mid-1966 as a new 1968 AMC car. Down the road, the American was to be all new for 1970, and so, from a production and marketing point of view, all AMC might need and could afford was in the hopper. Consequently, the two-seat V-8 sports car idea was shelved temporarily.

AMC President Roy Abernethy had no choice. In an effort to catch up with the 1964-1/2 Mustang, he had gambled—and lost—on the 1965 Marlin. AMC's slice of the automotive market fell from a slim 5.09 percent of total national sales to a meager 3.71 percent. The future of the smallest American car manufacturer looked bleak.

Enter four new men in top management at AMC. In the early part of 1966, these men rolled up their collective sleeves and tried to save an American car company literally on the skids to oblivion. By spring of that year, AMC Chairman of the Board Richard E. Cross was on the firing line. Stockholders felt he, and others in top management, were out of touch with the car market. The

The AMX had a grace and beauty in form that no other musclecar could match. This 1968 AMX is powered by a 390 V-8. It was one of a handful of two passenger, high-performance sportscars made in the U.S. The twin centerline white stripes designate the "Go-Pack." Adam Oritz

This is a factory cutaway of the 1968 AMX. Larry Mitchell collection

An original AMC Advanced Styling Studio drawing of the new 1968 AMX in its final form, just after actual production started. Larry Mitchell collection

This is the AMX introduction at Orange County Raceway in California in February 1968. Pictured is Indy winner Rodger Ward on the left, AMC V. P. Dick Teague in the middle, and an unidentified man on the right. Larry Mitchell collection

company was being attacked by the press for the same reasons, except the press was thinking of writing stories about the late, not-so-great, American Motors Corporation. There was speculation about a merger or a buyout to try and keep the Rambler boat afloat, but no one seemed to be interested. And then a knight in shining armor came riding in the front door on a white horse: Detroit financier Robert Beverley Evans.

Evans was a man known for healing sick and ailing companies, and giving them a vision for the future. Although not an auto man, he had automotive experience . . . and a good deal of money. He bought 220,000 shares of AMC, got a seat on the board of directors, and rattled the chains of those who had not kept in touch with the changing American car market. He had ideas the board liked, and he was soon made chairman of the board.

Evans knew AMC needed new cars, new engines, and a new attitude about the youth market and racing. His influence got the AMX two-seater idea off the shelf and into a committee to determine how they could make such an unusual car. The idea they came up with was simple: Since the Rebel was made from the Ambassador, why not

THE AMX STORY

The AMX Story *was a special full-color, eight-page brochure given out by AMC at dealers' showrooms. It was exclusively about the new, 1968 AMX and what the little sports car offered a buyer in fun and comforts.*

make the AMX from the new Javelin that was currently being engineered in Kenosha. The new Javelin was fairly cost effective, as it was based on the mechanics of the Rambler American. The new 290 V-8 was already in production, giving a more modern powerplant to the whole AMC lineup, and a 343 version and a 390 version based on the 290 were planned in the near future. Evans said the AMX was needed, if for no other reason than to give the company a unique two-seater sports car. It wouldn't quite be a competitor for the more sophisticated Corvette, but it would be much more of a personal-sports car than the Mustang.

The AMX would be a car to create excitement at the dealer showrooms and, above all, help

The 1968 AMX in rare Classic Black with a black interior. The luggage rack was a factory-approved, dealer-installed option.
Larry Mitchell

Matador Red with white stripes was a very popular color combination in the first year of production. The rally wheels in 1968 were fully chromed, 14x6-inch units with Goodyear Custom Wide-Tread Polyglas redline tires. **Adam Ortiz**

change AMC's image, which was a decade behind the times and out of touch with the younger car buyers. Evans made it clear to the board that a car like the Vignale AMX prototype could help change the public's image of American Motors. Since the Project IV cars interested a lot of people, perhaps making the Javelin and the AMX could help keep that momentum going. Ambassadors, Rebels, and future cars might be sold to a market that now wouldn't be caught dead in a Rambler showroom. AMC Engineering set to work to see how they could spin the AMX off the Javelin and still create two similar but different cars.

The ball was rolling, but both board chairman Evans and president Abernethy soon realized more changes were needed. Both men soon stepped aside and allowed new blood to take over and continue where they left off. Evans recognized the talents of Roy D. Chapin Jr. and promoted him from an executive vice president to take his place as chairman of the board. William V. Luneberg, who had been automotive group vice president, became the new corporate president replacing Abernethy.

Chapin knew AMC needed to get into racing and he sought out a man key to the whole new management team, Victor G. Raviolo. Raviolo had worked 20 years for Ford in various engineering and product planning positions, and he had a serious love for and experience in car rallying and racing. An unconfirmed rumor has it Chapin told Henry Ford II that he was hoping to get someone from Ford to fill a new slot at AMC. Ford supposedly said he doubted Chapin could steal anyone away, but Ford reportedly recommended Raviolo, who had had an excellent record with Ford and had the talents Chapin wanted, but was no longer with Ford. Raviolo had started his own consulting business in Detroit.

Chapin made Raviolo an offer he couldn't refuse and got him to join his new management team at AMC as a group vice president in charge of research, engineering, styling, and product planning. One of the first comments Raviolo made was, "I'm also very fortunate to have (Styling Vice President Richard A.) Teague and John Adamson (engineering vice president) and a lot of others. . . ." Raviolo eventually promoted in-house talent and ex-race driver Carl Chakmakian to performance activities director. This new management team was responsible for the turnaround in thinking at AMC and for implementing the new cars to come—the most unique being the two-seat AMX.

Raviolo and Chakmakian persuaded aftermarket performance manufacturers to make speed parts for the new AMC V-8s and that led AMC into racing. There was a complete reversal of the strong, national, antiracing stand AMC had taken in 1964. By the summer of 1967, with the introduction of the 343 V-8 option in the American (called the Super-Americans), the company known as Rambler became the new company of American Motors. That fall, dealer showrooms were attracting new, younger customers who wanted to see the new Javelins. A few months later, a car no one ever thought AMC would really build arrived as the little brother of the Javelin. The AMX finally went into production. It would later earn the nickname, "The Image Changer."

The 1968-1/2 AMX

The exciting new AMX sports car was unveiled to the waiting AMC dealers at nine meetings held in nine U.S. cities, starting on February 15 and ending on March 22, 1968. The intro meetings were held at Playboy Clubs and the theme of the shows was "Mission AMX"—a takeoff of the popular TV program, *Mission Impossible*. National Merchandising Manager Guy Hadsall Jr. was in charge. Preregistration by dealers for these shows doubled when Hadsall invited record-setting AMX drivers Craig Breedlove and his wife, Lee, to be guests of honor. The AMX introduction shows were a great success, and most AMC dealers were cranked up to get back home and sell this neat new sports car.

The 1968 AMX was unveiled to the automotive press in February 1968. The introductions took place where it was warm—one at Daytona International Speedway in Florida, and the other at Orange County Raceway in California. The press and invited dignitaries got to run AMXs around pylons and flog the 390 versions down

What made the two-seat AMX so attractive was the "flying buttress" roofline that extended all the way to the rear quarter panel end caps. It was fastback styling at its best. Adam Ortiz

This 1968 AMX is a four-speed with the rare Rally Pac gauges and hooded overlay. The door panels had a "V"-shaped woodgrained panel. The recliner lever for the seats is trimmed with a chromed plastic cover. Dan Behymer

This is a close-up of the 1968 factory-approved, dealer-installed Rally Pac. A 24-hour clock is on the left and an over/under oil/amp gauge on the right. Note the AMX dash number on the glovebox indicating an early-production car. Dan Behymer

Pictured here is a very early 1968 AMX with the Ford/AMC four-speed shifter with reverse lock-out collar. This car has no air conditioning nor Rally-Pac, hence the center dash panel above the radio is solid. Note the AMX dash plaque on the glovebox door. Larry Mitchell

the quarter-mile. This gave them a firsthand feel for the cars and a lot of fodder to go back home and write about the new AMX.

A drag race was held at the Orange County intro, and the press was invited to run the cars down the 1320-foot strip for a single, best elapsed-time trophy. The fastest time of the day was turned in by the man in charge of the show, Guy Hadsall Jr., who ripped off a 14.37-second quarter-mile with a trap speed of 93.65 miles per hour. His run put to shame the representatives from every major national car magazine. Hadsall had never drag-raced anything before until his blast with the AMX. Although it wasn't completely kosher, AMC gave Hadsall the trophy anyway.

Most of the major car magazines and newspaper tech editors generated full drive-reports and pictures about the car and, generally, they were very enthusiastic about this short-wheelbase, big V-8 package of dynamite. The 1968-1/2 AMX was a hit. *Car and Driver* said, "If AMC had done something as bright as the AMX five years ago, they'd be in a lot better shape today."

From Javelin to AMX

When the green light was given to make the AMX in September 1966, costs dictated that it had to share as much with the Javelin as possible, yet it had to look and feel different. The AMX was not intended to go head-to-head with Corvette. That would have been foolish and far too expensive, and GM wasn't selling that many 'Vettes anyway. A four-wheel, independent suspension would have cost AMC a major bundle of money, and the car would have to be at least equal to a 'Vette in ride, performance, and comforts, or get lambasted by all those who cherish the plastic fantastic. A direct challenge to the Corvette by little AMC could easily have been a major financial disaster, in which the stockholders would hold lynch parties over ex post facto. A car more like the 1955 Ford Thunderbird was the way for AMC to go—a personal, sports-luxury car.

The AMX also would have a twofold agenda: to attract attention *and* buyers. To attract attention, AMC made the AMX a unique sports car that was innately capable of generating a lot of press, then the company spent a lot of money on advertising and promotion. The goal: to change the image of American Motors from that of an old-fashioned bunch of Rambler fogies, to "hip," "with-it," "cool," performance guys.

The second AMX mission was to bring young buyers into AMC dealerships to buy either an AMX or a Javelin. The AMX was to be an automotive calling card linked directly to the sales staff. It was not a true bait-and-switch because if prospects wanted an AMX, they would be sold one. But rather than lose a sale if the customer felt two seats was fun to come in and look at, but not practical to own because of the wife and kids, a Javelin would be an excellent substitute. It was a classic spider-and-the-fly sales technique.

The 1968 AMX got its looks from the original AMX I mock-ups that became the 1966 Vignale AMX prototype Project IV show car. On the other hand, the 1968 Javelin got its looks from the AMX II, but it had a roofline more like the Vignale AMX. Styling elements blended with each other and the two cars wound up with many common styling traits. The 1968 production Javelin and the 1968 production AMX are both alike yet unlike. But both cars evolved from different prototypes brought to life, and both made their developmental siblings proud.

The AMX had to be produced from the Javelin's unibody and share its driveline and suspension components to cut production costs, speed introduction, and make an attractive sticker price to secure buyers. To create a two-seater sports car from a four-seater pony car, exactly 12 inches were sectioned from the Javelin floor pan just behind the front seats. This shortened the 109-inch wheelbase to 97 inches and completely eliminate the Javelin's back-seat area in the process. The V-8, front trunnion suspension, and rear axle of the Rambler American became the mechanicals of the Javelin and, thus, the AMX. Javelin doors, front fenders, front and rear bumpers, taillights, headlight doors, windshield, back glass, and trunk lid were all shared between the Javelin and the AMX. Grilles, hoods, roof panels, quarter panels, and side glass were different, however.

Inside, the AMX had the identical interior of a Javelin SST—the dash, door panels, front carpets, seats, steering column, and wheel were the same as the Javelin. Minor plastic trim, the headliner, and rear carpet differed. The engines were all the same, except the base AMX came with a 290 four-barrel and dual exhaust, while the Javelin made do with a 232-inch six. Four-speed transmissions and V-8 automatics were shared.

Although one might get the impression the Javelin and the AMX were much alike, they really were not. The AMX single inlet grille, power blistered hood, and convex rear roofline made for two cars that might be from the same parents, but looked quite different. Ride, handling, and performance were also close, but different enough to be felt. A 390 Javelin was dignified and restrained, while the 390 AMX was a little beast, an automotive Taz. Yes, the AMX had a character all its own.

This solid black 1968 AMX has the optional 390 V-8 and Go Package, but the original owner ordered the car from the factory with the stripes deleted. Larry Mitchell

The legendary AMX 390 V-8 introduced in the 1968 AMX is shown here. This engine was totally American Motors' own design. It produced big-block torque of 425 at only 3,200 rpm. All 390s had chrome valve covers, oil breather cap, and air cleaner lid. Dan Behymer

The single-venturi grille and the over-the-roof stripes gave the AMX a very different look from its sister car, the Javelin. The deeply recessed grille also gave the AMX a shorter overall look when the car was viewed from the side. Larry Mitchell

The AMX looked like the high-performance sports car it was, coming or going. Larry Mitchell

Few can deny that the 1968 AMX was one of the most attractive-looking cars of its time. Take away its sister car, the Javelin, and the AMX shared not one single line with any other car, including those made by General Motors, Ford, or Chrysler. The 1968 AMX was especially graceful and handsome when viewed from the broadside, where the indentation of the single-venturi grille made the car look even shorter than it was. The rear quarter panel treatment was simply a work of art. In fact, the AMX won a design award from the Society of Automotive Engineers (SAE). "Clean" and "sleek" are words used to describe the AMX. "Timeless" and "classic" are others that have come to be associated with it as well.

The fake inlets on the hood were mildly criticized by some automotive journalists, yet they were hardly as stupid-looking as what wound up on some cars of the time, like the fake chrome injector "stacks" on Super Sport Camaros of the same era, or the fake fender ports on various Buicks dating back to the late 1940s. The subtle, pressed-in ridges on the hood of a 1968 AMX were

This mildly customized 1969 AMX is the only American Motors product to ever run the famed Cannonball Sea-to-Shining-Sea Memorial Trophy Dash. This event was a timed run from New York to Los Angeles and was also, immortalized in a movie. This 343 V-8 AMX ran it three times. It has also competed in closed-circuit road races in Nevada, attaining speeds of 150 miles per hour. Bruce Jacobsen

neither as bold nor as blatant as bolt-on chrome geegaws used on some cars. To the eye, the ridges added a certain balance and accent. The same can be said for the kick-out around the rear wheel-house. Overall, the AMX is rather devoid of tacky add-ons, exemplifying the term "clean lines," which has been used by car people for decades to describe a simple, attractive design.

The Ramble seat did not make it into production. It was a nostalgic, passing-fancy idea that pending federal laws, product liability responsibilities, and common sense ultimately ruled out. Most feel it would have hurt rather than enhanced the looks of the car.

The new 1968-1/2 AMX was carefully targeted to a price well below that of a 1968 Corvette—nearly $2,000 less. AMC was clever to associate it with the Corvette, but not directly compare it to the 'Vette. The AMX came in 14 exterior colors and red, beige, and black for the interior. Unique, over-the-roof twin racing stripes dramatically

In 1968, AMC's Vice President in Charge of Styling Richard A. Teague had this 1/18th- scale model handmade by a European master modeler. It is of the Vignale AMX prototype with opening Ramble seat, doors, and hood. Hinges for the lift-up rear glass and doors and the wire wheels are crafted from metal. The detail is exquisite. Teague said he paid over $3,000 in 1968 to have the model done. Larry Mitchell collection

A 1969-1/2 AMX is shown in one of the most desired colors, Big Bad Orange. This car has been owned by this author for 30 years and has only 18,885 actual miles. The factory-approved, dealer-installed American Torque Thrust wheels were ordered on this AMX new. Larry Mitchell

Pictured here is a Big Bad Green 1969-1/2 AMX 500 Special. An unknown number of this color combination received a special plaque on the hood by the Southern California American Motors Dealer Association to commemorate a race at the track in Riverside. The wheels on this car are owner-installed Magnum 500s. Jerry Heasley

enhanced the looks of the car, greatly differentiating it from its sister, the Javelin. The stripes were a part of the performance Go Package, available only on the optional V-8s. Most AMX owners will tell you an AMX isn't an AMX without the twin stripes. The stripes screamed performance and gave the car distinction. The stripes were available in 1968 only in white or black.

A base AMX was still a performance car, even with the standard 290-ci, 225-brake horsepower V-8 under the hood. For the $3,245 base price, a buyer got a 290 V-8 with a four-barrel and dual exhaust. A Borg-Warner T-10 four-speed close-ratio manual transmission with floor shift was standard, but no console was available. The four-speed used a 2.23:1 first gear. Cheesy three-speeds weren't available, to prevent watered-down performance. The 290 and 343 V-8s got the Warner Gear M-11 automatic, first produced in 1958. Testing revealed that the big-block's torque caused clutch and input/output shaft failures, so a beefed-up version called the M12 was made for use behind all 390-equipped cars, AMXs included. It was the same case with a bigger clutch-pack, and it displaced one quart less fluid, which meant different dipsticks.

Mag-style hubcaps were standard, as were blackwall Goodyear Custom Wide Tread Polyglas performance tires. Inside, reclining bucket seats covered in vinyl, full carpeting, and a 120-miles-per-hour speedometer and tachometer were standard features. Headrests were optional in all AMXs produced before January 1, 1968, after which federal safety laws made them mandatory.

Optional to the AMX were the 280-brake horsepower 343-ci engine or the new "AMX 390" with 315 brake horsepower. Both were 10.2:1 compression, leaded premium–burning motors with a Carter AFB four-barrel and dual exhausts with chrome tips. The 390 motor was reserved exclusively for the AMX, and wasn't available in the Ambassador, Rebel, or Javelin at the start of the 1968 model year. This marketing ploy reinforced the "AMX 390" name, and announced that AMC was into serious, high-performance cars . . . even if it was a few years late.

All AMXs received rear axle traction bars that attached to the top of the axle and bolted to the rear subframe rail, plus a 3/8-inch steel plate was included inside the boxed section to reinforce the floor. The traction bars served two purposes: reducing axle hop and increasing roll stiffness. The bars eliminated rear axle hop under hard acceleration and severe braking by preventing the axle assembly from "winding up," making the AMX a more serious performance car than many others out at the time.

Shown is another 500 Special, this one with the Trendsetter Sidewinder sidepipes. This car is one of the best-restored AMXs in the land, scoring 99.5 out of 100 points in the classic AMX Club International Annual Concours. Jeff Mueller

The license plate tells the world this is one of fewer than 200 1969-1/2 AMXs painted in Big Bad Blue. Larry Mitchell

Some owners like the look of the 1968 all-chrome AMX rally wheel more than the 1969 painted version. This 1969 AMX looks super sharp with chrome "Magnum 500" wheels. Larry Mitchell

For 1969 the AMX 390 engine was painted Alamosa Aqua rather than the Caravelle Blue that was used on the 1968 engine. This 1969 engine bay shows quality and stock. The car is a four-speed because it has the mandatory smog pump. Jerry Heasley

The "torque links" also added a high degree of roll stiffness to the rear of the car, greatly improving handling over the Javelin, which used only staggered shocks for some axle tramp control. The arms of the links used fat rubber bushings squeezed between the mounts and were put under tension like a wound-up rubber band. The design worked well and the AMX went from initial oversteer (non-throttle induced) to typical Detroit mild understeer, at higher speeds than a Javelin. (Most agree the AMX still needed a larger front and rear sway bars together to give truly excellent handling, like Z-28 Camaros and Boss 302 Mustangs, but AMC offered nothing beyond the small front bar and the rear torque links.) The AMC Model 20 rear axle was used in the rear and was excellent for street and mild strip use.

The usual options were on a long list to jazz up the AMX, including power steering; power front disc brakes; air conditioning; tilt steering wheel; full tinted glass; AM, AM/FM, or AM/8-track stereo tape player; all-chrome 14x6-inch rally wheels; electric wipers (yes, AMC still used vacuum wipers); automatic transmission with full-length

All AMXs painted in Big Bad Colors had front and rear bumpers that were also painted, rather than the usual chrome. All Big Bad cars also had standard rear bumper guards. This car still sits on 30-year-old, original tires. Larry Mitchell

console; Twin-Grip limited slip (Dana Power Lok); and a host of lesser options.

The famed Go Package was a very popular option and consisted of either a 343 or 390 engine, power disc brakes, E70-14 redline Polyglas tires, higher-rate shocks and springs, Twin-Grip differential with 3.15:1 gearing for the automatic-equipped cars or 3.54:1 gears for the four-speed cars (2.87:1 and 3.15:1 gears were used on standard, non-Go–equipped cars, respectively), heavy-duty cooling (seven-blade fan and fan shroud only), and vinyl over-the-top racing stripes. A dealer-installed gauge pack was available that consisted of an oil/amp gauge and a clock. The Rally Pack, as it was called, was not available with air conditioning as both used the center dash panel above the radio for either the air outlets or the gauges. You could get one or the other, or neither, but not both.

Making The AMX Exclusive

Wells, Rich and Greene went to work to sell the American public on the AMX. It is not known for sure, but is thought that Mary Wells and her firm came up with the idea to give each AMX a dash plaque with a sequential number on it, not

A show-quality 1969 AMX interior in saddle tan with original leather seats shows the mottled effect the leather coloring had. This car has a factory Hurst four-speed shifter, the center fold-down armrest, and air conditioning. Note woodgrain on armrests, center dash panel, and doors, a new feature for 1969. Adam Ortiz

Shown here is the original charcoal leather interior of a 1969 AMX. This car has air conditioning, automatic transmission with the full console, and other small options accessories.
Larry Mitchell

unlike Shelby did with the Ford Cobras. The first 50 or so AMXs had a cast dash plaque that just said, "AMX." The plaques were mounted on the center dash pad above the radio. Then an engraved dash plaque appeared that said, "AMX 00001." It was mounted on the glovebox. A few hundred cars later, the number went back on the center dash panel. A bold statement was printed in the first 1968 full-line AMC catalog, which read, "Such a lot of car, we're only making 10,000 in 1968. We're even putting the production number on the dash—for collectors who want to prove they got in on a great car fast." This was a simple marketing ploy to give an impression of exclusiveness and limited numbers to try to garner quick sales.

(Note that the dash plaques were sequential for all three years and not matched to the VIN of the car, or anything else. At the end of the 1970 AMX production run, the numbers on the dashes were over 3,000 higher than actual car production.)

A separate, eight-page, all-color brochure called the *AMX Story* was produced and given out to AMC dealers. The whole brochure was about the AMX and nothing but the AMX. A number of other sales aids were produced to help dealers sell—and customers understand—the new AMX.

AMC knew 10,000 was break-even and since the car came out at midyear, they really could only make about 10,000 AMXs in that short period. They were also hoping the production lines would be running to capacity making Javelins, Americans, Ambassadors, and Rebels.

Car Magazine Reviews

The AMX was covered in every national car magazine there was in the spring of 1968. *Sports Car Graphic* splashed a banner on the cover of its March 1968 issue stating, "AMX—New Image Sports Car."

Pointing to the new AMC upper management team, they said, "We feel it important to make mention of this breath of fresh air blowing through the corridors of power in Plymouth Road, Detroit, just in case readers may find it difficult to reconcile the mainly favorable comments we make in this issue about the latest American Motors products with the less happy reports they may have read in the city columns of their newspapers concerning the company's financial fortunes. We would just mention that current balance sheets must still be affected by past errors in administration, but that in our view, with the combined virtues of the Javelin and AMX, American Motors has undoubtedly its best chance EVER of being pulled out of the red and firmly into the black."

The first paragraph of the road test portion of the article flatly states, "American Motors has engineered a very good car." And if *Sports Car Graphic* said the AMX was a sports car, it was! They tested the super-torquey 390 AMX and knew how to launch the car off the line to get honest quarter-mile times. The test car was a dead-stock 390 with the Warner Gear M-12, three-speed automatic, and a 3.15:1 rear end. They reached 0-60 miles per hour in 7.4 seconds; not overly exciting, but accurate for an automatic. The quarter-mile was up in 14.6 seconds at 91 miles per hour. The 0-100 test came in 18.0 seconds, showing the torque-based power the big AMC 390 had to push the not-so-aerodynamic 1960s musclecar through the air.

Motor Trend opened its road test of the new AMX asking, "Is the AMX a True Sports Car?" The answer was a strong "yes" in the American tradition, not the bugs-in-your-teeth, side-curtain English definition.

"Here comes image buster No. 2—and it fits neatly between the pony cars and sports cars," said *Car Life* about the AMX. They recorded a 14.7 quarter-mile time with a 390 four-speed AMX.

Car and Driver magazine quoted Teague in his description of the new AMX as the "hairy little brother to the Javelin." They went on to say, "(The AMX) is the first AMC car in recorded history that every enthusiast can own with pride and drive with pleasure." C&D had a 390 with the automatic

This is a 1969-1/2 AMX California 500 Special. Note the brass plaques on the power blisters of the hood. Larry Mitchell

in its test car and ran 0-60 in 6.6 seconds, 0-100 in 16.3 seconds, and a quarter-mile in 14.8 seconds at 95 miles per hour.

Testing an AMX for *Science and Mechanics* magazine, Joe Gutts said about the new AMX 390, "The big blaster of the bunch (the 390), while not anywhere near the 427 Vette, is hefty enough to warp the mind of any Mustang owners."

Cavalier magazine said, "AMX son of Rambler." Generally, AMC tried to distance the AMX and the Javelin far from the negative connotation "Rambler" had come to signify. They made it clear to the press that the AMX was not a Rambler. Mario Andretti was at the introduction at Orange County and with his high degree of skill, ran a 390 four-speed AMX to 0-60 in 6.2 seconds, 0-80 in 11.5 seconds, and 0-100 in 16 seconds. He said the AMX was, "a fabulous package at $3,300."

Without a doubt, the AMX was very well received by an automotive press that was generally negative about Ramblers for years. The press was also aware that the company had been losing money by pickup loads in the last couple of years.

National Advertising, Promotion, and Auto Shows

Ads by Wells, Rich, and Greene agency in car magazines shouted, "The AMX. It takes more than money to get one." Another ad warns the buying public, "The new AMX will be sold as democratically as possible." The ads were designed to create excitement and enthusiasm and a degree of exclusiveness to the new AMX. Most ads made reference to the AMX dash numbering.

Contests went on and were announced in magazine ads, not all of which were car magazines. *Look* magazine ran ads aimed at giving away four new 1968 AMX sports cars in a national drawing sponsored by the National Retail Hardware Association. They repeated the AMX sweepstakes again for 1969. Ads were run in national car magazines showing Breedlove's 1968 red, white, and blue race AMX at speed, setting 106 speed and endurance records.

AMX 1/25th Jo-Han scale promotional models were available at the dealerships (actually 1968 versions, but sold as 1969 models). Toy store Jo-Han versions were also made, put-together kits were available, and, eventually, slot car toys, Hot

The 1970 AMX was restyled from the cute appearance of the 1968–69 version into a more aggressive look for 1970. AMC V. P. Dick Teague said the marketing department of AMC wanted the car to have a hood scoop like most other American performance cars had at the time. Larry Mitchell collection

This is a modern-day 1969 AMX vintage-style road racer. This very streetable car has topped 170 miles per hour in sanctioned open road racing on Highway 318 in Nevada in recent years. Larry Mitchell

Wheels, and more. At your local AMC dealer or through the mail, one could get nylon red, white, and blue racing jackets; stickers; hats; and other novelty items with the AMX Racing Team emblazoned on them.

Craig Breedlove toured with the 1968 AMC new cars at the auto shows. The 1968 Chicago Auto Show was held from February 24 through March 3 at the International Amphitheater. The AMC display was dazzling. It featured the *Grant Rebel SST Funny Car*, the Breedlove record-setting AMX, a Frost White AMX, and a Frost White Javelin, both with the new AMX 390. Seven engines were on display, as well as Group 19 AMC performance

parts you could buy for your new AMX or Javelin. Breedlove was dressed in all white and ran a booth with a shifting contest. Participants got to shift a Hurst four-speed, trying to match a recording of Breedlove shifting his race AMX.

Special AMXs

Since AMC used the Playboy Clubs to introduce the new 1968 AMX, it was only fitting that owner Hugh Hefner give one to his 1968 Playmate of the Year, Angela Dorian. She was given a specially painted pink 290 AMX with rally wheels. Dorian still owns the car today, although it is now painted black.

Contrary to other sources that report 25 to 50 copies of a 1968 "Breedlove red, white and blue Street Replica" were produced, no information or documentation has ever surfaced to substantiate this claim. One AMX has surfaced, ordered new by a dealer in Canada, and it is being touted as a 1969 factory "Breedlove Replica" 290 V-8 AMX. There has never been any factory literature, order sheets, advertising, photographs, or anything else to properly document any factory 1968 or 1969 "Breedlove Replica" AMXs. It is likely this one car was simply a special-order car done in red, white, and blue at extra cost for the Canadian dealer to show and promote as he personally pleased.

It is noteworthy that a former AMC Kenosha plant employee said that special-order, multicolor paint jobs were not painted by AMC in Milwaukee, because there was no room to pull the bodies off the production line and do this kind of work. He said these vehicles were base-color shot in Milwaukee, then trucked to Kenosha as normal, where local Kenosha body shops did the final work in air-dry enamel.

Famous customizer George Barris was commissioned by AMC to whip up a bolt-on customizing kit for the 1969 AMX. The kit would then be sold through AMC dealers. His kit was called "El Toro" and consisted of a rear ducktail spoiler and wire wheel mags. In addition, stick-on decals provided contrasting color around the mouth of the grille, the power blistered hood, around the windows, and the AMX circle on the quarter panel. The grille was replaced with square mesh metal sheeting, not unlike the 1955 Thunderbird's stock grille. On the

This 1970 two-seat AMX sports car is shown in Matador Red with a white "C" stripe. The beautifully executed ram-air hood was standard on the AMX that year. Although more aggressive in looks, the new front suspension actually gave the car a more luxurious ride and feel. Larry Mitchell

The simulated side exhaust rocker panel covers from the 1969-1/2 Javelin option list became standard on the 1970 AMX. "Rebel Machine" 15-inch rally wheels became optional also. New taillights were shared with the 1970 Javelin to cut costs. Larry Mitchell

hood sat what Barris called "injector clusters" with 390 emblems. The rear of the car looked good with the spoiler; the rest of the car was simply awful. Only a few kits were sold, and today, they are rarely (if ever) seen.

Breedlove was tapped to also create a custom, bolt-on kit for the AMX to be sold through dealers. He came up with the AMX 200 on paper and the AMX 600 kit in reality. The "Aerodynamic" kit used a fiberglass front end with the nose and fenders molded together. Smoked plexiglass hid the headlights and grille and the 'glass hood had large, indented scoops. A roll bar was installed, and a version of the rear roof spoiler that Breedlove used on the Bonneville Speed Spectacular Javelins in 1968 was bolted to the roof.

Breedlove's kit was to retail for $700, less the American Torque Thrust mags and dash tach. It, too, was awful and few were sold, if any. One Super Stock AMX, called *The Sheriff of Nottingham*, has this kit on it today. It is owned by Bruce Nottingham, who was a team member on the Bonneville Javelins and who lived near Breedlove's original shop in Southern California.

Jim Jeffords was manager of the Javelin Racing Team and governed the team's efforts in the Trans-Am series. Jeffords personally liked the Ramble seat idea of the Vignale AMX prototype and thought it ought to have been produced on the 1968 AMX. He decided he alone was going to revive the concept and make it available as a special, custom AMX he named after himself, the Jeffords

AMX R, with the "R" being for Ramble seat. He bought a new 1968 AMX and had Puhl's House of Kustoms re-create the Ramble seat. He liked the results, but almost everybody else did not, including AMC, which told Jeffords they wanted no part of the idea, because of several objectionable traits of the car.

One objection was that the body work added over 600 pounds to the car, right over the rear wheels, which required much stiffer rear springs that sacrificed ride quality. The weight also drastically upset the car's handling in corners, braking, and acceleration. Climbing over the rear quarter panel to enter or exit the rear, flip-up seat was awkward and dangerous. Rear-end collisions could easily cost lives and create lawsuits. The seating was not comfortable and put Ramble seat passengers in the direct path of airstream coming over the roof. The added roof spoiler lip did nothing, and there was no communication with the driver from the rear seat. The whole concept and execution was really a fiasco and sure to be a loser at the sales desk.

Jeffords and AMC got into a major tiff about the AMX R, and Dick Teague said the company refused to sell him the cars to modify and eventually threatened to sue him if he built any more. AMC felt they could face major lawsuits out of injuries getting in and out of the Ramble seat, or

A special two-tone paint scheme was optional on all colors of the 1970 AMX, including Classic Black. This paint option was called the "Shadow Mask" and was ultramarine-type flat black paint across the hood, fenders, and around the windows like the mask of the Lone Ranger. The engine bay was also flat black. Unfortunately, it stained easily and trapped dirt. Larry Mitchell

"Group 19" is the 19th of 28 sections of the AMC Master Parts Catalog. The Master Parts Catalog was used by the parts department of each and every AMC dealer in the United States and Canada. Each section has to do with a major area of the cars AMC made. For example, Group 1 consists of all the parts that make up the various configurations of the AMC six-cylinder and V-8 engines. If a customer or dealer service department needs a set of pistons for a 390 V-8, the pistons have a specific part number and are listed for the model and year application in Group 1 of the Master Parts Catalog. If one needed an alternator, door panel, or taillight lens, they can be found listed in their proper Group section of the AMC Master Parts Catalog.

Group 19 in this catalog has to do with high-performance parts that were available for various AMC models and engines. This section first appeared in the 1966 edition of the AMC Master Parts Catalog for the 1967 model year run. It contained all the high-performance, aftermarket equipment that was being made for American Motors cars. AMC never offered any of these speed parts from the factory.

All Group 19 parts were ordered by the dealers or the car owners from the dealer parts department, which sent the order in to the area zone depot. It was the zone depots that inventoried most of the Group 19 parts, not the main Milwaukee AMC parts warehouse. All high-performance parts listed in the Group 19 section of the parts book were assigned official AMC part numbers. But all parts were made by aftermarket manufacturers that sold AMC parts carrying the genuine AMC part numbers—or sold the same thing mail order or at local speed shops without the AMC part numbers. (Some items, such as camshafts, did not carry AMC part numbers, because there was no space to put a number on the part to be used inside an engine anyway.) The fact that AMC did not install any speed parts on their cars from the factory has always hurt those who have raced AMC cars, especially in the early days. Most SCCA Solo racing rules allow such things as aluminum high-rise intakes and Holley carbs for Ford, GM, and Chrysler cars because many models of their cars, including the Z-28 or Boss Mustang, came with that kind of high-performance equipment right from the factory. At AMC, those parts only came *dealer-installed.*

So, the Big Three racers can run those things, but the AMC boys cannot. This fact always disappointed this author, who tried to race AMC products in SCCA events 30 years ago. If AMC had offered the Donohue Javelin or Trans-Am Javelin Replica with *factory-installed* aluminum intake, Holley carb, cam kit, headers, wider rims, and other high-performance parts, it would have made things much easier for those in spirited amateur competition to race and win, especially road racing and autocross. But the Group 19 parts were always outlawed, and under the rules of protest by the Big Three drivers, few AMC cars had a snowball's chance. Once a Camaro driver got beat by an AMX and found out the AMX driver had an aluminum intake, he protested to the track officials and the AMX got put into a modified or pure race class, where 427 Corvettes and the like would eat them for breakfast. Not many AMC owners wanted to turn a needed daily driver into a trailered pure race

Group 19
AMC High-Performance Parts

car, let alone contend with the huge monetary resources needed to compete with the Corvettes and Shelby "R" Mustangs that dominated the tracks.

Why did AMC do things that way? Hard to tell for sure, but a couple of theories come to mind. First was the AMC five-year/50,000-mile warranty. Little AMC took a big gamble offering such an extensive warranty, but it had to instill consumer confidence in its products. If it made Javelins, AMXs, or Americans equal to Z-28s and Boss 302s or even Shelby Mustangs, they could suffer a major loss of image to the youth market they were after if the special high-performance cars they factory-built blew motors and shelled transmissions—which was likely, as the (new) AMC drivers tended to be less skilled in performance driving for a number of reasons. In addition, AMC engineers knew the AMC V-8s were excellent motors, but were not of the same caliber as the Z-28 and Boss motors. AMC designed the V-8s in 1965 for passenger-car use, not racing, like other motors from Chevy and Ford. The final reason is that AMC drivers had a tendency to hammer the cars harder to keep up with or beat the Big Three cars, and this took a higher toll on the cars that cost the owners, AMC, or both, money and reputations. So, AMC sold AMXs, SC/Ramblers, Donohue Javelins, T/A Replica Javelins, Machines, and the like, with dead-stock motors.

If you wanted more performance than stock, you bought speed parts over the AMC counters or aftermarket—and your warranty was voided on the engine if you so much as installed a Holley carb or a set of headers. AMC wanted a racing and performance image, but could not factory-back your new AMC car with a warranty if you built up the engine. Some dealers would provide a warranty, but only a handful. Most owners bought the Group 19 parts from local speed shops, because they cost less than AMC wanted over the parts counter. Many dealers took orders for Group 19 parts and obtained them locally from the speed shops, sans AMC part numbers, because they could make a better profit than by ordering them through the AMC zones.

Early Group 19 290, 304, 343, 360, 390, and 401 V-8, high-performance parts included the following: a hydraulic camshaft and kit (Crane); a blocker heat riser intake manifold gasket; a four-bolt provision (Donohue) for 1970-up 360-ci blocks; a single four-barrel, medium-riser, dual-plenum, aluminum intake manifold (Edelbrock R4B); a Cross Ram, dual four-barrel, medium-rise, open-plenum aluminum intake manifold (Edelbrock STR-11); dual-point distributor with or without mechanical tach drive (Mallory Double Life) with hi-po coil (Mallory); ring-and-pinion gear sets 3.73:1, 3.91:1, 4.10:1, 4.44:1, and 5.00:1 (AMC-cast and machined); V-8 Torque Link kits (AMX rear axle traction bars); front underbody spoiler for the AMX or Javelin; rear deck wing spoiler (Kaplan-made); forged cranks and/or forged rods for the 290 and 343; 390 cast-iron steel single four-barrel intake manifold; capacitor discharge ignition system (GM Corvette L-88); adjustable roller rockers (Crane); and positive-locking differential (Detroit Locker). These were most, but not all of Group 19, factory-approved parts, but not the dealer-installed hi-po parts.

The two-seat AMX from 1968 through the end of AMX production in 1970 was a foot shorter in the wheelbase than its sister car, the Javelin. The 12 inches were taken out behind the front seat, leaving no space for a rear bench seat as this photo shows.
Larry Mitchell

as a result of rear-end accidents, or loss of control due to the excessive added weight. Another AMC concern was warranty claims on early mechanical failure due to the massive extra weight.

Only 6,725 1968-1/2 AMXs were sold and given away in 1968. The selling season was less than five months.

Upscaled 1969 AMX

Since the AMX came out at midyear, AMC had no plans to do anything except refine the car for 1969. A lot of running changes were made to the 1968 AMX and into the 1969 model year. It is a fact that AMC was surprised that 1968 sales failed to reach the 10,000 unit break-even figure, especially in light of the amount of publicity and advertising the car got during that half year. But Javelin sales were good, which took some of the sting out of the disappointment.

Still, it was a painful and costly lesson for AMC that the lack of respect among the young buying public couldn't be easily nor quickly reversed—even with excellent performance and cars as gorgeous as the Javelin and AMX. And for those who lived the times, a lot of potential new car buyers shunned AMC cars because they still felt the company was going down the tubes and they would be buying a dead horse. When an AMX or Javelin would beat a Big Three car at the strip or on the street, it was an embarrassment to the Big Three driver, who still called them "Raaammbllerrs" (said it with scorn and sarcasm), downing the cars. On the street or even the strip, animosity toward AMC cars wasn't cured by the AMX or the Javelin—and in most cases, it only got worse.

AMC listened to complaints about the Spartan look of the 1968 AMX interior and addressed them with a simulated woodgrain finish for new armrest overlays, the center dash panel above the radio, and the consoles of automatic-equipped cars. Door panels on 1968 cars had a wood-grained "V" on them for accent, while the 1969 panels got a square woodgrained accent, which dramatically enhanced the appeal of the interior. Then, AMC went the opposite way in covering the entire seating surfaces in Ventilair vinyl, making the seats look like cheap seat covers from a discount store.

For those who couldn't accept the look of the vinyl seats, genuine leather was offered for the first time in 1969 as a $79 option in charcoal and saddle tan colors. The vinyl colors for the year were basically carryovers: red, new charcoal instead of black, saddle tan instead of beige, and a new color, platinum, which was a silver-gray. At the start of the model year, 12 exterior colors were offered, and Matador Red and Frost White were popular carryovers. Over-the-roof stripes continued in carryover black and white with three new colors added, red, medium blue, and silver. The beautiful all-chrome rally wheels made by Motor Wheel were now painted "charcoal glitter" and took a stainless-steel trim ring.

The base 290 AMX remained the same. The option list only had a couple of additions: leather seats and "Command Air," which was a three-speed fan with center outlets where the air-conditioning outlets would otherwise be. This was in answer to complaints about the 1968 "Flow Thru" ventilation that didn't.

Outside, the AMX saw no changes to any sheet metal except the inner hood panel, which was stiffened due to stress cracks that developed on the 1968 models. Inside, a new, large tachometer that matched the speedometer was in the instrument cluster opening to the left, with a 140-miles-per-hour speedometer on the right. The small opening to the far left now took a blockoff plate or a clock, instead of a small tach. In midyear, a visor was added to the plastic overlay covering the main gauges to help block glare and to also make the dash a tad better-looking. AMX dash numbers continued to be placed on the center dash pad above the radio.

The carpets went from loop to cut pile (some late 1968s had cut pile), and the new smooth headliner replaced the waffle-patterned Kivar 1968s, a running change into early 1969. The gas pedal went from being a hinged unit to an improved suspended style. Chrome trim was added to the parking brake, clutch, and brake pedals. A new grab handle was installed above the glovebox door on the dash.

Complaints about no console for the four-speed cars went unanswered, but a small plastic change tray was installed between the seats and a useful center fold-down armrest was optional between the seats on the four-speed cars. In midyear, an OEM Hurst Competition-plus four-speed shifter took the place of the AMC/Ford unit for those who had to have a beefy lever to jamb the gears with and strip the synchros. Engines, transmissions, and rear axle ratios all remained unchanged for 1969.

The same wild colors offered on the Javelin for 1969-1/2 became available on the AMX also—Big Bad Orange, Big Bad Blue, and Big Bad Green. Over-the-top stripes came in black or white if the Go Pack was ordered. One could get a 290-powered 1969 AMX in any Big Bad Color, without stripes; 284 were made orange, 283 green, and 195 blue. Today, the Big Bad Orange 1969-1/2 AMX is the most sought-after color of any AMX of any year, followed by Matador Red models.

New 1969 Ads

Mary Wells and her advertising team continued their creative ads for 1969. One two-page print ad showed an AMX on one side and a blank space on the other, with a headline that read: "An unfair comparison between the AMX and . . . what?"

Another two-page 1969 ad showed a 1957 Corvette and a 1957 Ford Thunderbird with an AMX in the middle. The banner read, "The first American sports car for under $3,500 since 1957."

Special AMXs

The Southern California Dealers Association ordered a number of Big Bad Green 1969-1/2 AMXs with tan leather interiors, all 390, Go Pack cars with black stripes. Most were automatics with air conditioning, though some had four-speeds. A special bronze plaque with crossed flags and the words "500 Special" was affixed to the power blisters on the hood. These cars were replicas of the AMX used to pace the 1969 California 500 Indy car race at Ontario Motorspeedway in California. After the race, they were offered for sale at AMC dealers in Southern California. It is unknown how many were ordered and sold, but it's a good guess that there were between 50 and 100 produced.

For 1969 the AMX was chosen to be the official pace car for the 47th annual Pikes Peak Hillclimb held on June 29 on Pikes Peak near Colorado Springs, Colorado. The Denver-area AMC dealers made one car the official pace car and ordered about 15 matching AMXs to be loaned to name drivers as courtesy cars during

The ram-air hood on the 1970 AMX (and Javelin) was closed off to the outside unless the Go Package performance option was ordered. Note the ram-air ducting on the underside of the hood with the vacuum line going to the flapper that opened the duct to allow outside air to the air cleaner when the throttle was depressed. Larry Mitchell

the week of the race. All cars were Frost White with red stripes, red interiors, 390 engine, Go Pack, and, it is thought, automatic transmissions. The cars were sold though local dealers after the race.

Only one car—the one driven by Bobby Unser as a courtesy car—survives today. It is owned by Dennis O'Shaugnessey of Chicago.

AMI (Australian Motor Industries) bought 24 AMXs in knocked-down form and assembled them in Melbourne in 1969. AMI fabricated a right-hand-drive dash and other components and used upholstery of its own. The cars were offered in only three exterior colors.

Shipped to Australia, built, and converted, they cost double the same car in the United States and each ran a 343 engine with an automatic.

In 1969, Remington Rand held a contest offering new, red, 390, four-speed, Go Pack AMXs as part of a national give-away contest. Ads were run in national magazines showing a shaver with the dial in a certain position. Anyone who could match the example found at a Remington dealer or an AMC dealer could win one of the cars. How many cars were given away is unknown.

Last of the Breed—1970 AMX

The 1970 AMX got a facelift inside and out. The hood was changed to make the car slightly longer and give it ram-air. All four fender/rear quarter extensions were new, but were shared with the Javelin. New taillights and a redesigned front bumper were also shared with the Javelin. Even the ram-air hood was shared between the two models, although it was optional on the Javelin. On the outside, fenders, doors, quarter panels, deck lid, rear lower valance, roof, and rear bumper remained the same as the 1968–69 AMX except for the side marker light holes in the quarters and fenders. The window glass was the same as the 1968–69 AMX, except the 1970 got a new Chemcor, thin windshield that defrosted quicker and broke into granules with no sharp edges in an accident. Exclusive to both 1970 cars were their grilles.

Inside, the 1970 AMX shared the Javelin's dash, with the exception of unique overlays to each car. Door panels were the same, as was the console for automatic-equipped cars. Front carpets were the same, though the rear sections differed,

The 1970 AMX received a complete new dash with a large woodgrained overlay that swept across the face of the dash from door to door. The "rim-blo" steering wheel was also new, as were the high-back, nonreclining bucket seats. This car has the optional Command Air ventilation system and leather seats. Larry Mitchell

as did the headliners, but they were the same as the 1969 AMXs and Javelins in each respective 1970 model.

Engines, drivelines, and suspension were also shared. In fact, making a 1970 AMX from a 1970 Javelin required only a few exclusive parts, including the shortened floor pan for the AMX. Noticeable cosmetic changes were wanted for the 1970 Javelin by AMC. Since the changes were not going to cost a fortune, and with the two-seater AMX scheduled to disappear after 1970, the changes were billed to the Javelin and the 1970 AMX got them for free, just to see if more aggressive styling would turn buyers on and increase sales over 1969 AMX figures. Hopes were up for the 1970 Javelin, too.

Teague said that his styling studio wasn't responsible for the new, bold looks of the 1970 AMX (or Javelin)—AMC's Marketing Department was just following what all the other pony and muscle-car-makers did to make their cars look more "macho." The ram-air, power blister hood treatment was a perfect example, and was arguably one of the best-looking hoods from any carmaker.

Colors again changed from the 1969 AMX with Matador Red and Frost White as third year carry-overs. Over-the-roof stripes were replaced with side "C" stripes that were optional and were not a part of the Go Package. A special two-tone paint treatment called "Shadow Mask" became optional and used flat black paint that went across the upper surfaces of the hood and front fenders, and around the side windows. The engine bay was also flat black. This paint looked good, but stained easily, and since it was quite porous, it trapped dirt. The 14x6-inch 1969 charcoal glitter rally wheels became standard, while the "Rebel Machine" 15x7-inch wheels were optional.

Interior colors were black, tan, and red leather or vinyl with an additional color of blue vinyl. Standard were the Ventilair breathable vinyls with the leather optional. Reclining low-back bucket seats with adjustable headrests were replaced with high-back, nonreclining buckets. Simple pleats were used on the center sections of the seats, leather or vinyl, and had matching door panels. The dash was entirely new, although similar in layout to the 1968–69 units. A flat, full-length wood-

grained aluminum overlay with the letters "AMX" was used, along with the AMX dash plaque located on the glovebox door. Consoles on automatic-equipped cars remained the same with a new, lockable lid. There was still no console for the four-speed cars, but the nice armrest between the seats was a carry-over option. The GM Saginaw steering column incorporated the key in the column and was lockable when the key was removed. The new Javelin SST "rim-blo" steering wheel was standard and connected to a variable-ratio power steering unit that replaced the 1969 fixed-ratio box.

The new twin balljoint front suspension copied from the 1968 Ford Mustang and standard on the 1970 Javelin was thereby standard on the 1970 AMX. Although touted as being "high performance," it actually gave a softer, more luxurious ride over the trunnion system. Modified for racing, it had antidive capabilities, but the street version still allowed the front bumper to head for the ground under hard braking, no matter what the sales literature said. The AMC Model 20 solid rear axle sat on leaf springs.

The standard engine was the new 290-brake horsepower 360-ci V-8 with new Motorcraft (Ford) four-barrel and dual exhaust with angle-cut chrome tips. Optional was the 325-brake horsepower 390 with the Motorcraft four-barrel and duals. A lot of internal improvements were made to the 1970 motors, including new block castings for a higher deck height and stronger 1/2-inch head bolts. "D-port" or dogleg heads with log-style, dogleg exhaust manifolds were used. Most of these improvements came from AMC's racing adventures.

The Go Package consisted of either the 360 or 390 motor with the functional ram-air hood (nonfunctional otherwise), power front disc brakes, F70x14 Polyglas SRWL tires, handling package (heavy-duty shocks and springs), Twin-Grip differential in selected ratios, and a heavy-duty cooling package with a seven-blade fan and shroud.

All the comfort and convenience options available on the 1969 AMX were available on the 1970 AMX. The 1970 AMX had gone the way of the then-current Mustang and had be-come more of a luxury-oriented performance car, taking on a quite different character than the 1968 and 1969 AMX.

Car Magazine Reviews

Many national buff magazines badly panned the 1970 AMX, despite all the mechanical improvements. Some beat up on the 1970 AMX until it was painful to read. They didn't like the new, more aggressive looks; they thought the interior was cheap-looking; and they didn't think the handling was that good. Most liked the power of the 360 or 390, though. *Road Test* magazine always liked AMC products, and it tested a 1970 AMX and actually liked the car. *Popular Hot Rod* ran a 360 four-speed AMX with the Go Pack through the quarter in 14.90 seconds. *Super Stock and Drag Illustrated* berated the car inside and out, but liked the 390 engine and cut a 14.46-second quarter-mile with its four-speed car with the optional 3:91 Twin-Grip rear. Very good, but not overly impressive, considering the refined engine with a rather low rear gear. (Like the Javelin, the 1970 motors badly needed the "free-flow" exhaust manifolds that were one year away.)

The year of the big-block on the streets of America was 1970, and performance engines from Ford, GM, and Chrysler had more cubes and as much as 100 horsepower more than the 1970 AMX. The last year of the AMX was a distinctive, macho-looking car that greatly appeals to some collectors today, but some still like the 1968–69 model better in roughly the same ratio as the cars sold when new.

Sales of the 1970 AMX were an embarrassment with just over 4,000 finding buyers. Unfortunately, 1970 AMXs got nailed with a surcharge by some insurance companies, which helped nix sales. New, unsold 1970 AMXs were leftovers at some AMC dealers into 1971. One Iowa dealer finally sold his leftover Big Bad Blue 1970 AMX in the spring of 1972.

Advertising

AMC knew the 1970 AMX was the last year, and that some buyers would be scared off at buying the last of anything. They had tried to jazz up the car with mean looks and tried one last time to get to the magic 10,000-unit sales figure. Full-color ads in car magazines showed a Matador Red 1970 AMX with white "C" stripes. One ad stated, "A sports car for the price of a sporty car," pushing the base price of $3,395. Another ad headlined, "We made the AMX look tougher this year because it's tougher this year." The text outlined the new changes to the car and tried to make a case for the aggressive looks. It did look svelte and mean.

A total of 4,116 new 1970 AMXs went home with new owners. Considering how many millions of people in the United States and Canada could have bought a new car in 1970, and how many did buy Camaros, Mustangs, Challengers, and the like, it was a sad ending to the most unique production car to ever roll down the AMC Kenosha assembly line—one of only a handful of high-performance American two-seat sports cars ever made.

At the end of the three-year run, 19,134 two-seat AMXs had been sold—10,866 short of break-even and far under what AMC had hoped for. It was not as if American Motors didn't try.

Beyond the AMX-AMX/3

The 1969 AMX/2 show pushmobile was enough of a hit with the American public that AMC decided to embark on a project to actually make a limited number of cars to finally try to convince the world the company was reborn from its Rambler days and could design and build exotic sports-performance cars. The plan was to build and sell a revised version of the AMX/2, to be called the AMX/3. It was to be a sleek and fast midengined vehicle using the 390 V-8 for power.

Knowing they could not afford to make dies and build the swoopy sports car in Kenosha, AMC contracted with Italian custom coachbuilder Prototipi Bizzarrini in Livorno, Italy, to hand-build the cars and ship them to the United States to be sold through AMC dealers. This wild idea was doomed from the start. AMC initially stated that it wanted to make 5,000 a year, but reality soon set in. Considering handmade construction time and costs over a few months, the figure was revised down to 2 a month or 24 a year. The original target price was $10,000 to $12,000, but again AMC realized that making the car and shipping it back to the United States in such low numbers was going to push the retail price to as much as double that. At $20,000 in 1969, there would be virtually no buyers for such a beautiful, but overpriced car.

AMC still went ahead with the making of a few cars that cost nearly a quarter of a million dollars each. The body panels were hand-hammered into shape by old-world Italian panel beaters and then welded together.

Five completed cars were eventually completed before the contract was canceled. A few unfinished bodies were ordered to be destroyed, but one car near completion was finished, making a total of six running cars. Five AMX/3s are in the United States and one is in Italy. An operational, fiberglass-bodied AMX/3 has recently been reported to exist in California, but that rumor, as well as any details about it, could not be verified by the publishing date of this book.

Each of the six 1970 AMX/3s that were completed had minor external differences that were implemented as running changes, but each was powered by the lightweight, yet powerful AMC "Rebel Machine" 390 with its 340 horsepower, which was isolated in a compartment right behind the cockpit. An Oto Melara four-speed transaxle was used with German-made four-wheel disc brakes. The car had a 105-inch wheelbase, weighed 3,100 pounds, and was only 43 inches high.

The estimated top speed was 160 miles per hour, but it was proved that the cars became airborne at around 125 miles per hour. I know, I drove one that fast. If the car had a set of wings, I know she could fly!

The cars had other problems that could never have been worked out over such a short production run. The cars ran hot with the engine in the rear and the radiator up front. Shifting was accomplished with rods that ran nearly four feet from the shifter next to the driver to the transaxle behind—one shifted the car with the sureness and precision of a Corvair. Additionally, engine heat vented from slots in the hood came up over the hood and right into the side windows, and using the air conditioner only hurried up the 390's eventual overheating. The handmade bodies had no rustproofing and the paint had to be thick due to the hammer marks in the sheet metal. Finally, the speedometers all ran backward due to a misunderstanding between the Italians and Stewart-Warner.

Still, the AMX/3 stands for all time as the most breathtakingly gorgeous car AMC had ever created in form and in function. It died because it was a far too wild and crazy idea from a company as small as AMC. No one at AMC seems to have done any homework on costs, and we will always wonder how much Teague influenced the building of the AMX/3 just to fulfill a personal dream. Within one month of the introduction of the AMX/3 in July 1970, Ford Motor Company hit the market with a hybrid De Tomaso Mangusta with a 351 Cleveland Ford V-8 for a price that the AMX/3 couldn't come close to. The Ford Pantera used an existing (limited) production car, the Italian Mangusta outfitted with Ford power. This venture is not unlike what Shelby did to make the Ford AC Cobra in the 1960s. It is amazing AMC management thought they could have an exclusive and exotic body handmade in Italy, shipped to the United States, distributed, sold, warranted, and make money at an initial price of $10,000–$12,000.

six

SC/Ramblers, Machines & Hornets, Oh My!
Wild, Wonderful AMC Creations

There were those at AMC who longed to make up for mistakes made on the 1967-1/2 343 Rogues—those who lamented the fact that American Motors was holding funeral services for the Rambler name and the Rambler American itself as a long-produced and well-known car.

These hard-core Ramblerphiles, lurking in the hallways on Plymouth Road, had a plan up their sleeves to give the American a send-off the automotive world would never forget.

If General Motors had Doctor Oldsmobile, AMC had Doctor Frankenstein. And one day came those words: "It's alive, it's alive." It was the day the 1969 SC/Rambler was brought to life!

1969-1/2 Rambler SC/Rambler

AMC already had George Hurst on the payroll for racing and product consultation. Hurst was considered a part of the Javelin Racing Team. He was even given the ultimate honor of a red, white, and blue Brill Brothers AMC leather racing jacket with his name on it. Fewer than 30 people ever got one of these beautiful jackets, and most were involved in AMC's racing efforts.

It was a "gimme" to get Hurst and his Hurst Performance crew to work a 1969 Rambler American Rogue into a performance street sweeper. They had created the 53 mighty 390-powered drag-race Hurst Super Stock 1969 AMXs and another, minor project would be a cake walk. Walter Czarnecki of AMC and Dave Landrith of Hurst are the creators of what was the most visually outlandish factory musclecar ever produced by a major factory. The new car's performance more than made up for the mistakes of the 1967-1/2 343 Americans.

The Rambler Hurst SC/Rambler was first shown at the Chicago Auto Show on March 8, 1969. Even in an ocean of performance iron at the

The mighty 1969-1/2 Rambler Hurst SC/Rambler "A" Model had just about the most bold graphics and paint scheme ever seen on an American musclecar. The car was intended for street and strip use and to give the Rambler American name a final tribute in spades. Bruce Jacobsen

The AMX 390 V-8 fit easily under the hood of the SC/Rambler because the engine bay had the same dimensions as the AMX and the Javelin. Larry Mitchell

The engine badge was moved from the rear quarter panels to the front fenders to intimidate drivers of other brand musclecars at the stoplights. The blue-painted rally wheels were a part of the bad-to-the-bone paint scheme. Larry Mitchell

show, the car made waves. Some laughed, some swooned, and some were just stunned. The little Rambler American two-door hardtop Rogue with an AMX 390 under the hood and painted bodacious white, red, and blue with blue rally wheels could not be missed by those walking around at the show, nor by the automotive press. It said, "Race me if you dare." It was Drag City for quarter-mile junkies.

The basic Rogue hardtop was beefed up in the floor pan to handle the 315 horsepower of the AMX 390 and the abuse a manual four-speed would do to the factory weld joints. The excellent AMX Torque Links were adapted to the American and linked the rear axle to the frame to eliminate axle tramp and also to add roll stiffness for improved handling. Disc brakes up front were standard, while drums soldiered on in the rear. The AMC Model 20 rear axle with 3.54:1 Twin-Grip could handle the power, as could the V-8 driveshaft. All normal Rogue badges were eliminated inside and outside.

The AMX 390 easily dropped into the engine bay of the American, because the bay had been redesigned in 1966 for the 290 V-8, which has the same external dimensions as the 390. An AMC/Warner Gear T-10 four-speed with heavy-duty clutch and an OEM AMC/Hurst shifter topped with a Hurst T-handle allowed for easy rowing through the gears. Dual exhaust with loud Thrush-brand glasspack mufflers and bologna-sliced chrome tips completed the mechanicals.

On the outside, things got hairy. The SC/Rambler was basic white and devoid of Rogue side trim. The centers of the sides were painted bright red with a 390 emblem on the front fenders and a special plastic badge that read "SC/Rambler/Hurst" on the front fenders (and rear taillight panel). These tags gave the cars in the other lane a serious warning. Both emblems installed on the front fenders had to have been done by a street racer who knew the intimidation factor street racers driving a Big Three car would experience as an SC/Rambler eased up next to them at the stoplight. The only way an SC/Rambler driver would be intimidated was if the car in the other lane had hood tags that said Hemi or W-30, or 455 HO. SC stood for Supercar and the H for Hurst.

A Grumpy Jenkins–style hood scoop that looked like a laundry detergent box painted white was turned on its side with one end open and pointing up. The pointing up was to really get a breath of fresh, cool air from the stream going over the hood and ram it down the throat of that Carter AFB four-barrel. When it did, it leaned out the

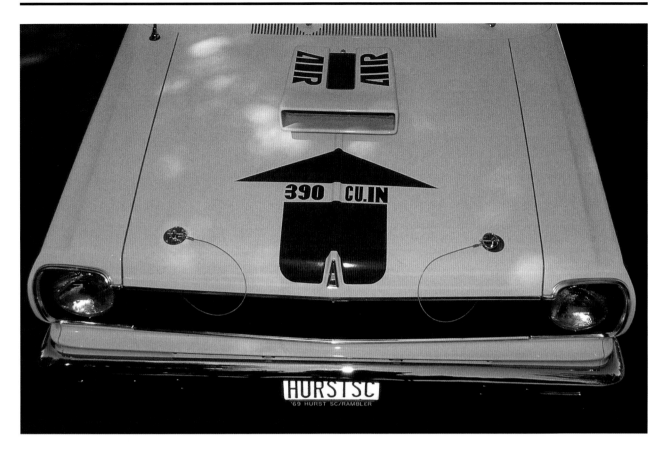

Incoming cold air knew it was to go into the gigantic hood scoop and into the torque-producing, all-AMC 390 engine. Larry Mitchell

air/fuel mixture, but who cared about function when form was everything.

Beyond the hood's scoop, SC/Ramblers had to have hood pins, since all true musclecars were so fast they could overpower the hood latches and flip the hood over the roof at speed. Hood pins were real race stuff, so the SC had them. A blacked-out grille gave a performance look, and the redline tires were mounted on *blue* rally wheels. Thrush mufflers with woodpeckers painted on them provided minimal restriction.

If all this weren't enough to get attention, Czarnecki and Landrith added blue striping and red lettering to tell the incoming air where to go—up the hood, into the scoop, and into the 390. Any excess air could follow the blue striping over the roof and be gone. The Talbot-style English racing side mirrors on the doors looked out of character with the car. Mirrors like these were seen on mid-1960s styling mock-ups in Dick Teague's Advanced Styling Studios, but it's doubtful Teague suggested the use of them on the drag-race-oriented SC/Rambler.

The interior of the SC/Rambler was plain, but meant for quarter-mile business with the Hurst four-speed shifter with its "T" handle and the Sun tach hose-clamped to the steering column. Larry Mitchell

The "B" Model SC/Rambler toned down the graphics due to the "A" Model intimidating potential buyers. It was still an all-American Motors musclecar and could not hide in traffic behind a Checker cab. Bruce Jacobsen

AMC Vice President in Charge of Product R. W. McNealy looks at the SC/Rambler with Hurst Performance President George Hurst at Orange County Raceway in California. Larry Mitchell collection

Inside, the SC/Rambler was so plain and simple it was almost painful. The car was going to be made on a limited scale (linked directly to its ability to sell) and available at a selling price of just $2,998. Buyers got a performance bargain and an intimidating, attention-grabbing look for a bargain-basement price, but a very taxi-like interior. The seats were wide, individual, and reclining, but were not buckets, so they couldn't hold one in place as might be expected in a high-performance car. Plus there was no room in between them for a comfortable armrest for the shifting arm. Furthermore, the interiors were all drab charcoal gray, devoid of much trim, accents, and plain vinyl, except for red, white, and blue striped headrests. The car had dead-stock instrumentation, except for a Sun tach held onto the steering column with a stainless hose clamp, but there were no oil or amp gauges. An AM, push-button radio was optional. After all, hard-core drag racers can't hear the radio over the squealing tires; only the cruiser crowd listens to tunes.

The SC/Ramblers were sent to selected AMC dealers who had guts enough to put one on the showroom floor and weren't afraid to shock grandma and grandpa, who had bought a 232-six-powered four-door Rebel last year and were in for an oil change. A special display came with each car and consisted of a cardboard triangle display for the roof and printed sheets that matched the tops of the fender contours and were affixed to the car with double-faced tape. These items listed all of the groovy features the SC/Rambler offered, such as the AMX 390 motor, disc brakes, and the like. Single-page, two-color flyers were stacked on the hood and a prospective buyer took one.

AMC whipped up 500 cars to test the waters. Customers didn't break the doors down to get into the AMC dealers to see them, but they certainly attracted attention, including the local cops who busted civilian test drivers for the loud pipes.

A bulletin was released to dealers that said, "The SC/Rambler is the ideal vehicle for the motorist who wants better than average performance and also a car that is uniquely different from 70 million others on the street today." It goes on to state, "the car is designed for the motorist who wants a customized car, but has neither the time nor inclination to build it himself." Another bulletin stated all SC/Ramblers would be built identical with no equipment optional to prospective buyers. If you wanted bucket seats or automatic transmission, you were out of luck.

The 1970 Rebel Machine was created as yet another "image changer" AMC musclecar. The Machine was more of a family-oriented factory hot rod. It had a pumped-up 390 under the hood and could be optioned as the owner desired. Larry Mitchell

The interior of the Machine had genuine bucket seats and could be ordered with a Hurst-shifted four-speed or automatic transmission. The automatic-equipped cars had a full-length console. Larry Mitchell

Subdued graphics that told the world this car was something special were on the front fenders and rear end. A ram-air scoop with tach graced the hood, Pontiac style. Larry Mitchell

Wells, Rich, and Greene created a national magazine ad for the car that showed a SC/Rambler, described its features, and then bragged it would rip up the quarter-mile in 14.3 seconds—impressive for a dead-stock street car, showing major potential for those who would install bolt-on speed parts. At $3,000, the car was cheap as dirt.

Reaction to the first 500 cars was somewhat negative. Test drivers liked the power, loathed the interior, and were, themselves, intimidated by the bold exterior. A second run of 500 was done without the blue decals with red lettering and the red two-toned sides. These toned-down 500 SC/Ramblers only had a narrow red and blue striping just above the rocker panels. Sales were slow, which surprised AMC, but enough went to buyers that a third run of 512 cars was made. (AMC could have produced 3,000–4,000 and probably would have if they had sold.) The last 512 were just like the first 500 with the bold paint and graphics back. The character of the car production ran from Dr. Jekyl to Mr. Hyde and back again. The first and last red-sided SC/Ramblers are known as the "A" model paint scheme, while the middle 500 have the "B" model scheme.

In the end, only 1,512 buyers came into AMC showrooms to buy a new 1969-1/2 SC/Rambler across the United States and Canada. This is out of a few million American cars made and sold that year by the Big Four.

The SC/Rambler fell into a category of cars that were basically economy cars meant for a typical American family of husband, wife, and two kids. The American's basic peers included Novas, Falcons, Darts, and Valiants. Since the SC/Rambler was an economy car on steroids, it compared directly with the Dart 340 GTS, the Dart Swinger 340 or 383, the Nova Super Sport, and eventually the Duster 340.

Car Magazine Reviews

Car Life magazine took a new SC/Rambler out and ran a 14.20-second quarter-mile at 100.8 miles per hour. They loved the brakes, which they said pulled one G on Polyglas tires, and the handling wasn't bad at all for a small, family sedan-type hot rod.

Road Test magazine loved the car and the price, but balked at the two-tone A-scheme paint and the brash headrests. They were able to cut the lights just right and came up with a 14.14-second quarter-mile time at 100.44 miles per hour.

Car Craft mustered a 14.34 quarter.

Super Stock and Drag Illustrated magazine recorded a 14.31. The SC/Rambler would do just what the AMC ads said it would do. Imagine: a car company that did not cheat, didn't blueprint, port, and polish heads on cars before giving them to the car magazines to test, *and* only boasted of impressive drag strip times that the production cars could actually back up.

Even more amazingly, with the AMC Group 19 cam; R4B aluminum intake; 780 Holley carb; curved, stock distributor; headers; and a small set of slicks, the SC/Rambler ran 12.67 for *Super Stock* magazine. One private drag-racing team got its Scrambler to run a best of 12.10 with nearly the same modifications, but everything was a simple bolt-on—the engine never came out of the bay and was not blueprinted nor tricked out in any way. A lot of SC/Rambler owners blew away the competition at the drags, especially in NHRA F/Stock. A lot of 335-horsepower, 383-ci Road Runners, and 396 Chevelles were trailered by 390 SC/Ramblers. On the street, a lot of Big Three cars simply avoided lining up at the stoplight with a Rambler SC/Rambler.

The 1974 Matador coupe with a smogged 401 V-8 could still run the quarter-mile in the 15-second range dead stock. The bold and slippery styling came from NASCAR racing. The ultimate Matador coupe would be with the "X" trim package as this car shows. Larry Mitchell collection

The 1971 Hornet SC/360 coupe was AMC's last effort at making a musclecar that could beat insurance regulations. The car was just about as quick as the 390 SC/Rambler because of engineering improvements made to the 1971 motors. Larry Mitchell

The 1969-1/2 Rambler Hurst SC/Rambler ranks as just about the wildest high-performance car ever to come out of Detroit, and certainly out of Kenosha. Just like Butch Cassidy and the Sundance Kid, the 1969 Rambler American went out of production with six guns blazing in the face of overwhelming competition. At least in legend, it is coveted today by those who love its Rambler namesake and history, and who can take being seen on the streets in a car that looked like a Barnum and Bailey circus wagon. For 1970 the American was replaced by the all-new Hornet. The Rambler SC/Rambler didn't sell well, but it did make an impression on a lot of drag racers, street racers, and the press.

The Rebel Machine

AMC knew they had to keep the ball rolling on its new image. And it had promised the general public and stockholders that it would introduce one new car model every six months for five years, starting with the 1968 Javelin. Although it didn't keep track of them openly, we assume the Javelin was 1st, the AMX 2nd, the SC/Rambler 3rd, the Trans-Am Replica Javelin 4th, the Donohue Javelin 5th, the Machine 6th, the AMX/3 7th, the Hornet 8th, the Gremlin 9th, and the SC/360 10th.

What was needed to keep the promise was another performance car to keep up the turnaround image and to try to compete with the Big Three's cars. And it should continue the name of George Hurst working with AMC on project cars, even though Hurst was pretty much out of the AMC picture by the time the 1970 Rebel Machine came out. Somehow, Detroit ad guru Jim Wangers of Pontiac fame had a hand in the Rebel Machine.

Intermediate cars sold well to the young, performance-oriented buyers and this included Chevelles, GTOs, GS Skylarks, Cutlasses, Road Runners, and Super Bees. These cars were family sedans on megavitamins with big motors. Trouble was, the biggest motor AMC had was the medium-block 390, which made "only" 325-brake horsepower. By 1970 the floodgates of corporate control opened wide, and GM allowed major-league big blocks in its intermediate-sized cars to make 1970 the most fire-snorting, tire-burning, gas-guzzling year in American automotive history. Cars such as

This Gremlin has an owner-installed 390 V-8 under the hood and a four-speed on the floor. It replicates the Randall 401-XR Gremlins. The car runs mid-13 quarter-mile times, even at altitude in the Mile High city of Denver, Colorado.
Larry Mitchell

the 454 Chevelles, 455 Pontiacs, and 455 Oldsmobiles were let loose on the American youth in love with more and more power. They joined 426-, 427-, 428-, 429-, and 440-ci Chrysler and Ford products. The Year of the Big Blocks was 1970.

AMC had the Rebel scheduled for a 390 V-8 that had slightly bigger exhaust manifolds, a unique four-barrel intake manifold, a Motorcraft four-barrel carburetor, and 2.25-inch exhaust pipes with low-restriction mufflers. These gave the 390 the most street horsepower of all the AMC engines before and after. The Rebel Machine 390 sported an advertised 340 horsepower and 430 pounds-feet of torque. It was brute power, but no match for the locomotive strength of the big blocks from the competition.

The Rebel Machine was a rather large family sedan, a base Rebel two-door hardtop with a warmed-over production 390 V-8. AMC knew they had made a mistake by not offering customers a choice of options on the SC/Rambler, and so they opened up the option book on the Machine.

A buyer could order the car in any of the 16 regular 1970 AMC car colors. With the 16 regular colors, the hood was painted satin black. A special option, code number 768, gave a buyer a Frost White Machine with 3-M reflective red, white, and blue striping and a painted blue hood and lower rocker panel area, which is the most-recognized combination on the Machine.

Three interior colors were available in Ventilair vinyl, while vinyl tops were available in a choice of colors. Power steering; an automatic transmission with a full-length console; center armrests color keyed or red, white, and blue; air conditioning; and a host of other 1970 Rebel options could be had just by checking the order form. Rebel Machine buyers could have their car the way they wanted it.

Certain features came standard on the Rebel, and there were other features standard as a part of the Machine package. A buyer could choose between a Warner Gear T-10 four-speed manual transmission with Hurst shifter or a Warner Gear three-speed automatic. Twin-Grip limited-slip could be ordered as well as standard rear gears of 3.54:1 for the four-speed cars, and 3.15:1 for the automatics. A 3.91:1 was available on the Machine and select other 1970 AMC performance models, factory installed for the first time. Deeper gears down to a 5.55:1 were Group 19 and dealer installed.

Machines all had a special fiberglass, bolt-on hood scoop with a built-in hood tach. The scoop had the usual flapper valve that opened when the

gas pedal was floored. The Machines all received what was to be called the "Machine" 15x7-inch silver rally wheel with the infamous, nonremovable trim ring. Special "Machine" insignia graced the front fenders, the rear trunk lid, and the glovebox. It is not fully documented where the name (The Rebel) Machine came from. The use of the word "Machine" to refer to a car had been around for a long time, though. "She's a cool machine" dated back at least a decade.

Detroit publicity man Jim Wangers had a hand in the Machine project and promotion. Wangers had previously helped Pontiac by inspiring the creation of the GTO, then later with the infamous car magazine ad that even inflamed the federal government, let alone the insurance industry, by showing a GTO looking for a drag race on Woodward Avenue. Wangers liked hood tachs, because the driver didn't have to look down to see a tach when racing. Wangers must have thought hood tachs were "safer." AMC credited Hurst Performance Research with the concept of the car, but no Hurst badges are on the car as there were on the SC/Rambler. Something was going on that has not yet come to light, historically.

Someone also decided to use Rebel station wagon rear coil springs to raise the rear of the car in the air for a nose-down 1950s "raked" look. Or was it a 1960s jacked-up, air-shocked look?

Whoever did it must have thought the look would increase appeal to the young performance crowd. In reality, it threw the balance of the car off from front to rear and hurt the overall handling somewhat. A rear bar from the station wagon was installed to reduce the tendency of the rear end to oversteer and the car to do donuts when trying to hustle it around a corner.

The 1970 Rebel Machine was a more toned-down AMC high-performance model than the SC/Rambler and even looked quite good in the cloned red, white, and blue version . . . or a solid color. Matador Red with the black hood and a black interior with the silver wheels was a striking combination.

The 3,650-pound car was introduced to the high-performance buying world in Dallas at a drag strip on October 25, 1969. A cute slogan was created for the car: "Up with the Rebel Machine." A cartoon character not unlike one used by a major national gasoline company was seen in print ads and was even available via mail order from AMC. It had a hippie-looking guy with striped pants and long hair riding a unicycle gear (gearhead rather than pot-head?) and carrying a protest-style sign that read, "Up with the Rebel

This 1979 Pacer Limited V-8 wagon is a replica of a CGE or Diablo Pacer. It has the rare flare kit allowing large 245x15 Comp T/A radials and a 401 under the hood. It will hit 140 miles per hour in the top-end floor. This car is owned by the author. Larry Mitchell

Machine." It was an attempt by AMC to make the Machine look "hip."

Wangers' print ads for the car were honest, yet laced with humor. The most recognized was one showing a new tricolor Machine with copy that read, "For instance, it is not as fast on the getaway as a 427 Corvette, or a Hemi, but it is faster on the getaway than a Volkswagen, a slow freight train, and your old man's Cadillac." The ad is an automotive classic.

Car Magazine Reviews

Road Test magazine seemed to always wave the performance flag for AMC and it did so with the Rebel Machine, when it tested a red, white, and blue version with the optional 3.91:1 Twin-Grip rear and a four-speed. The car tipped the scales at 3,800 pounds—after all, it was an intermediate family sedan—but the car also managed a very respectable 14.57 elapsed time at 92.77 miles per hour for the quarter-mile. AMC said the car would do the quarter in 14.4 seconds at 98 miles per hour, and this was close enough considering AMC must have had an experienced drag racer run the claimed time.

Hot Rod magazine made some Group 19 additions to a Machine, including the standard fare of cam, carb, intake, headers, and slicks, to cover the major mods. With the 3.91:1 rear sporting a Group 19, gear-driven, nasty Detroit Locker, their best time was a 12.81. Not bad for a rather large car that was not slim and trim at just under two tons.

Owner 390/401 conversions are easy and fun. Imagine the looks on the faces of modern BMW owners when they get their doors blown off by this 401 Pacer. The car sports an incredible 72-inch-wide front track. Larry Mitchell

Production figures do not all agree, but published in the book, *The Hurst Heritage* by Robert C. Lichty and Terry Boyce, 2,326 total Machines were built, the first 1,000 of which were red, white, and blue. Unfortunately, it was another AMC musclecar that may have helped the image of AMC but didn't earn the company a dime in profits.

Special Package Matadors

The Rebel was renamed the Matador for 1971 and a revised "Machine" Go Package was made available as part of a 360 or 401 four-barrel engine option on any 1971 Matador two-door hardtop with any other equipment. It consisted of dual ex-

haust, 15x7-inch, slot-style steel rally wheels, E60x15 Polyglas white-lettered tires, Space Saver spare tire, handling package, and power front disc brakes. A four-on-the-floor or a floor-shifted automatic were the tranny choices. There was no Machine identification or other unique badging on the car inside or out.

A street NASCAR equipment package (consisting of minor cosmetic changes, including NASCAR decals) was also reported to be offered on the 1971 Matador hardtop in conjunction with the Go Package to try to garner sales of the Matador, which was being raced in NASCAR by Penske and Donohue with AMC backing. None have ever surfaced, however, indicating the effort did not meet with much success.

In 1972, AMC sold 500 fleet Matadors to the Los Angeles Police Department. The LAPD chose the cars after extensive testing of Chevy, Ford, and Chrysler police car offerings, because, the LAPD said, the Matadors outhandled and outperformed all the other cars. And the LAPD surely loved the power of the AMC 401s under the hoods. In one car magazine, a 1972 401 Matador police car and a 1972 401 Javelin both ran the quarter-mile in the 14.7-second range with the cop car only a tenth of a second slower than the sporty Javelin.

All cars were fleet/police 401 V-8s with automatic transmissions and heavy-duty fleet/police components. Most of the cars were black-and-white four-door sedans, though some cars were painted mundane 1972 AMC colors for detectives and undercover use. The LAPD and other law enforcement agencies ordered 1973 Matadors for police work, as well.

After being retired from many miles of duty, these 1972 and 1973 Matador police cars were sold for salvage at auction in Southern California. Many can be seen crashing in the *Police Academy* movies and on television shows made in the mid-1970s.

In 1974, AMC unveiled the unique-looking, bug-eyed Matador coupe. Both beautiful and bizarre at the same time, it could be ordered as a performance car of the times with the "X" package and a 401 V-8. This was to prove to be a one-year combination, as the mighty 401 AMC V-8 was retired from passenger car use at the end of the 1974 model run, though it continued on in the AMC/Jeep line until 1979.

A 401 Matador X weighed nearly 4,000 pounds and was choked to death with smog equipment typical of dirty, carbureted engines of the times. Only a column or floor automatic transmission was available.

Car Magazine Reviews

Super Stock and Drag Illustrated magazine tested a dead-stock, low-compression, smogged-to-the-hilt, 1974 Matador X coupe and ran it down the quarter-mile drag strip. In a headwind, they got a best run of 15.38 seconds at just under 95 miles per hour. For a 1974 car, the timeslips were simply unreal. But they *were* real.

The 1971 SC/360 Hornet

True to their word of one new car or model every six months for five years, AMC whipped up a special performance edition of the 1971 Hornet two-door sedan. Insurance surcharges, federal smog laws, and growing public outcries had brought the American musclecar to its knees, and it looked like the end was near.

As the big-block factory hot rods had compression ratios reduced to comply with the new pollution regulations, performance dropped dramatically. Former quarter-mile times in the hallowed 14-second bracket crept into the 15-second-plus mark.

AMC V-8s began to have an edge, and pulled even with many low-compression big blocks. The lowering of compression hurt the AMC V-8s, but not nearly as bad as most GM, Ford, and Chrysler V-8s.

In the midst of all this power downsizing, AMC made its last real musclecar. Based on the new, lightweight Hornet with a 360 two-barrel or 360 four-barrel, the car was badged in the decals on the front fenders as the SC/360—a Super Coupe with a 360 V-8.

For a starting price of only $2,663, the base SC/360 was equipped with the 245-horsepower, two-barrel 360 V-8, single-exhaust, three-speed manual transmission, floor-shift (no console), heavy-duty clutch, 14x6-inch eight-slot, styled steel wheels, less trim rings, D70x14 Goodyear Polyglas tires, Space Saver spare, custom steering wheel, individually reclining seats, red reflective rear valence trim panel, and exclusive SC/360 wraparound side stripes. One could enhance the car with such options as Twin-Grip, air conditioning, cloth inserts on the seats, and so on. The SC/360 was offered in any exterior or interior color any other Hornet had except for the Gucci designer interior that was only available on the Sportabout.

If you wanted to spend a few more bucks to make sure you could kick the tar out of that pesky 302 Maverick Grabber, Nova SS, or Swinger 340, a buyer could pop for the 360 Go Package. For the extra money, a buyer got a 285-horsepower 360-ci V-8 with four-barrel and dual exhaust, hood scoop with functional ram-air, in-dash tachometer, handling package with D70x14 Polyglas white-lettered tires, but there were still no beauty rings on the slotted, steel rally wheels and no gauges to keep tabs on the motor, only idiot lights. Optional with each of the 360s was a column-shifted automatic (no automatic on the floor) or four-speed manual with Hurst shifter.

The SC/360 was not made as an SC/401 because of insurance surcharges and the public outcry against young people dying in drag-racing–related wrecks on the streets in their Detroit-built high-performance vehicles.

This AMC Eagle wagon has to be considered a musclecar since the Canadian owner installed a 401 V-8 under the hood. The car uses AMC/Jeep driveline parts including axles. The Eagle surprises a lot of people, both on and off road. Larry Mitchell

The ads for the SC/360 were sane and honest. Gone was the bragging about quarter-mile times due to a major toning down of performance. Ads said, "Introducing a sensible alternative to the money-squeezing, insurance-strangling muscle-cars of America. The Hornet SC/360." The ad concluded with, "As a leading car magazine has said, 'the day of the heavy 400-cube, 400-horsepower supercar may be just about over' "—a prediction that soon came to pass.

Car Magazine Reviews

The four-barrel version of the SC/360 Hornet would easily dip into the high 14-second range at the drag strip. With a set of open headers, a decent set of tires, and some traction bars to help control minor wheelhop, *Car Craft* magazine had a best run of 13.78 seconds that also broke into the magic above-100-miles-per-hour range (101.92 miles per hour). This performance was 0.04 seconds faster than a 454 Chevelle *Car Craft* had just tested at the strip, and a 340 Demon with open

headers ran a best of 13.61—both were very impressive cars.

It should be noted that the compression ratio of the AMC 360 was a low 8.5:1 and the Demon 340, a very high 10.5:1. The Chrysler 340 was underrated at 275 horsepower and the AMC 360 over-rated at 285 horsepower. As an educated guess, the 340 was probably closer to 325 horsepower; most Chrysler fans would not argue with that amount of compression. The AMC 360 was 290 horsepower in 1970 with 10.0:1 compression, and a drop of 1.5 points of compression would put the brake horse-power closer to 250. Given 10.5:1 compression, there can be no doubt the SC/360 would have smoked the Demon like a breakfast sausage.

Like all the other AMC special models made from family sedans, the Hornet SC/360 didn't catch on with buyers—only 784 were built and sold, of which only a handful exist today. One reason the Hornet might not have sold well was the fact it was a two-door sedan, viewed by many as a return of the grannymobile Rambler American.

Hornet, Gremlin, and Pacer V-8s

The 1970 Hornet offered a 304 V-8 with two-barrel carb and single exhaust. In 1972 a 360 V-8 with two-barrel carb and single exhaust was offered in the Hornet line, which included the Sportabout.

Starting in 1972, AMC offered the two-barrel, 304 single-exhaust V-8 in the Gremlin. In 1977, AMC offered a Hornet AMX, in 1978 a Concord AMX, in 1979 and 1980 a Spirit AMX, all with an available 304-ci, two-barrel V-8. These cars were certainly lively in performance, but were not considered musclecars in the same way as the Hornet SC/360. They do make fun conversions to high-performance 360s, 390s, and 401s, though.

Dealer Conversion Cars, Big V-8 Gremlins, Pacers

Randall Rambler in Mesa, Arizona, did conversions on many AMC cars and Jeeps over the years. You could call Randall up from anywhere in the country, order up a new Gremlin X with a 401 V-8 custom installed by them, and fly out to pick it up a month later.

The Randall 401 Gremlin could be had as an automatic or a four-speed and most had decals on the side of the upper quarter panels that read, "401-XR" (X for Gremlin X, R for Randall). A stock 401 in the lightweight Gremlin produced a nasty little street rocket capable of mid-to-low-13-second quarter-mile times with good street tires and low restriction mufflers. *Car Craft* tested a 401-XR with bolt-ons of a cam, carb, intake, headers, and ignition system. They said the totally streetable, daily-driver Gremlin did a best of 12.22 seconds at 115.97 miles per hour. The 2,850-pound beast on a 96-inch wheelbase was a serious handful, but what fun you could have at the strip or on the street with a kammback cutie as quick as a flash of lightning, and wearing an AMC label. A 401-XR went for around $3,600, nearly double the price of a base Gremlin.

Randall also built 1975–76 Pacer coupes with an AMC 360 grafted in, and eventually would do a 401 conversion to customer order. They were like the conversions Don Yenko did at his Chevrolet dealership with 427 Camaros and Novas.

Lipman Motors, an AMC dealer in Hartford, Connecticut, put together a 360 V-8 Pacer coupe with the lettering, "Diablo" in the front doors above the rocker panels.

How many of the Randall or Lipman conversions were ever sold is unknown. Since a buyer had to pay the sticker price of the new Gremlin or Pacer and then for the costs of the bigger V-8 conversion, which ran $1,500 to $3,000 additional, not many could have been sold. Getting your con-

An owner-converted, 401-powered Gremlin is owned and drag-raced by Mark Ripley of Washington state. Mark Ripley

verted AMC car serviced and warranted at your local AMC dealership back home was a serious problem also.

A young Californian, Carl Green, wanted to get into custom cars in the early 1970s, so he created a 1975 Pacer coupe with flares and wide tires, was a hit with the public, and even AMC took note. He then met AMC Vice President Dick Teague, who liked Carl and gave him a new 1977 Pacer wagon to play with. Carl cut the rear roof off and welded on a Chevy Luv pickup rear cab panel, rounded the corners, and added his wheel flare kit and made the neatest-looking Pacer "El Camino–style" pickup you could ever imagine.

CGE tried to sell fiberglass flare kits through AMC dealers, but only a handful were ever made and sold. Lipman Motors did use them on its Pacer conversion called the Diablo, and Randall Rambler did make a few Pacer coupes and wagons with and without the V-8 and the CGE flare kit.

Armed with a simple fact, a lot of AMC owners have created their own AMC musclecars. The fact is the AMC V-8 family of 290, 304, 343, 360, 390, and 401 engines are all basically the same size on the outside, so a 304 can be removed from the engine bay of a Gremlin or a Spirit, a Hornet or a Pacer, and a 401 just drops right in. With an AMC A727 three-speed automatic, a more modern 700R GM four-speed automatic, a T-10 four-speed, or even a more modern Mustang five-speed (some mods required), one has a home-built AMC hot rod. (Yes, it does require a V-8 AMC Model 20 rear axle to take the power.) Swapping a smaller AMC V-8 with a bigger one has been going on for over 30 years.

seven

AMC Racing
Beating the Odds

Starting in 1964, Rambler openly shunned corporate and independent racing. The driving-age baby boomers who created the new youth market were told to go somewhere else to buy a high-performance car—and they did. Rambler management gambled they could survive with the older clientele who adored the company's product. The new Mustang shook the automotive world, and the company making Ramblers in Kenosha soon saw the writing on the wall. A nosedive in car sales and company earnings from 1965 and into 1966 forced a management change at corporate headquarters in Detroit. It was an overwhelming uphill battle to cut the losses and do an about-face in corporate carmaking philosophy. New models were needed, a new image had to be cultured, and racing was the only way to prove the company philosophy had changed to accommodate the new, young, performance-minded buyers. It was also necessary to prove AMC had cars as good as anyone else and engines and drivelines better than many.

By 1967 the "new" American Motors Corporation was born and was off to the races for the first time. Since 1967, a multitude of AMC owners have raced AMC cars. We respect and acknowledge all of their racing efforts in drag, road, circle track, and other forms of racing. However, space allows us to cover only the most prominent and well-documented AMC racing endeavors.

AMC's first full year of racing on tracks across the United States and Canada was 1968. New AMX and Javelin owners found the spirit of competition against Ford, General Motors, and Chrysler cars invigorating and stimulating. If an AMC driver won, it was raspberries to the Big Three owners. If an AMC driver lost, it didn't hurt. One was expected to lose driving a "Rambler." But winning with an

Stock-car driver Don White pilots a Kaplan-prepared 1968 Javelin Trans-Am race car at a special race held at the Daytona International Speedway in 1968. The event was not a part of the Trans-Am series but offered publicity for American Motors. Ronnie Kaplan is talking to driver Don White. Larry Mitchell collection

109

The only time two AMC Javelins held pole position was at the Mid-Ohio Trans-Am in the 1968 season. Drivers are John Martin on the pole and Peter Revson second on pole position. John Martin collection

AMC was far more cherished and savored than a Chevy beating a Ford or a Mopar beating an Oldsmobile. Those who have experienced the thrill of victory know that it is an amazing feeling, and they will never forget their AMC-powered victories the rest of their lives. The year of 1968 was the start of the underdogs getting long-overdue revenge. It has been a fun ride, to say the least.

The AMC Trans-Am Odyssey

The SCCA (Sports Car Club of America) had created a road race series called the Trans-Am for "Trans-America" or across America. The series had both privateers and factory-backed race teams running highly prepared race cars based on production. The series limited the type of cars that could qualify on major details such as wheelbase. The 109-inch-wheelbase Javelin qualified; its brother, the AMX, could not qualify due to its 97-inch wheelbase. The Trans-Am Series was a run for bragging rights as the Manufacturer's Championship Winners.

The teams had to be privately owned, but could be sponsored in research and development funding by any major car company with a car that qualified. The cars that competed in the 1967 Trans-Am series' over-two-liter class were the Chevy Camaro, Ford Mustang, Dodge Dart, and Mercury Cougar. For the 1968 season, Mercury pulled the Cougar out and American Motors jumped in with the Javelin. Pontiac entered the Firebird, but with a Chevrolet engine. This was legal since the Firebird was sold in Canada with a Chevy motor, and Pontiac had no small-block motors capable of racing at that time.

Ex-racer Ronnie Kaplan of Chicago was picked as the new Trans-Am Javelin Racing Team Captain, and Jim Jeffords was the team owner/manager. Jeffords had raced a Corvette called the *Corvette Purple People Eater* and won the SCCA B-production title in 1958 and 1959. Jeffords chose race car builder Kaplan Engineering to make race cars out of the production Javelins being built 50 miles north of Chicago in Kenosha, Wisconsin. It was Kaplan who first painted an AMC race car in hash red, white, and blue and blue, white, and red. They were the 1968 Trans-Am Javelin race cars.

Peter Revson jumped from his 1967 Mustang to pilot a new Kaplan Javelin. Camaro driver Craig Fisher came aboard the team along with George Follmer, Skip Scott, and Jerry Grant. John Martin from Antioch, Illinois, who had been racing a Rambler American in SCCA A-sedan, was recruited by Kaplan to convert the Javelins into race cars.

Martin quit his job as a mechanic for a local Chevy dealer and became crew chief for the team. He and Fred Duray were the men who hammered and welded the Javelins into race cars. Martin brought firsthand experience to the new Javelin Racing Team from building and racing his successful 1967 American in SCCA A/Sedan. The first year, Kaplan, Martin, and Duray turned AMC's 290 V-8 into a race motor. Contrary to what AMC stated in print 30 years ago, Martin said in a December 1999 interview that all AMC racing motors were done in-house at Kaplan Engineering, and Traco Engineering of California had no involvement at that time.

The 1968 Kaplan-built AMC 290 engine was 304 ci and produced 375 horsepower. (The class limit was 5,000 cc or 305 ci.) The very first Trans-Am race the new Javelin Trans-Am Racing Team competed in was Sebring in Florida. Drivers Follmer, Revson, and Martin covered 193 laps and finished 13th overall and 5th in the Trans-Am portion of the dual race event. Another Javelin was entered and raced by Janet Guthrie, Liane Engermann, and Bill Haenett. It finished 33rd.

For the June 16 Mid-Ohio event, Follmer was late because he was racing an early Indy-car event at Mosport. Team manager Jim Jeffords gave the Number 16 Javelin to team crew chief John Martin, who went out in the car he built and, amazingly, put the Javelin on the pole for the race. Peter Revson followed by qualifying his Team Javelin car as second fastest. For the first time, two tricolor

The new 1970 Mark Donohue Javelin race car is pictured here. The car was fielded for American Motors by Penske Racing and was sponsored by Sunoco and Sears Diehard batteries. Mark Donohue, himself, did the driving. Tom Benvie collection

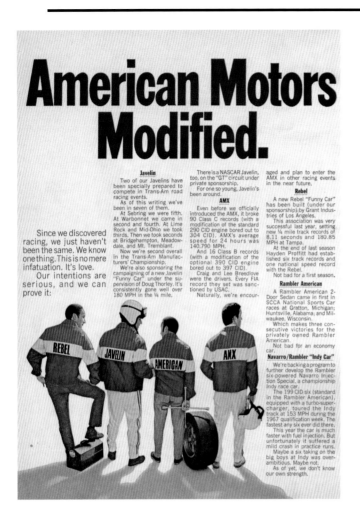

American Motors Modified.

This ad was run in select national car magazines in the fall of 1968. The ad is historic, as it announces to the world that American Motors is jumping into serious racing. This ad counters the antiracing Rambler ad of 1964 that severely hurt the company's image, but the 1968 ad was probably too little, too late.

American Motors Javelins sat at pole position for the start. They didn't win against the Penske Camaro with Mark Donohue driving, but one did cross the finish line. The Mid-Ohio race put some fear into all the competitors of the Javelin.

The AMC Trans-Am 305 V-8, single four-barrel (Edelbrock R4B aluminum medium-riser intake)–powered Javelins raced against Camaros and Mustangs with dual-quads for the first part of the 1968 season. Ronnie Kaplan made a special trip to Vic Edelbrock's shop in California where they created the AMC/Edelbrock "Cross Ram" dual-quad aluminum intake. The SCCA legalized the Cross Ram to give the AMC Trans-Am 305-ci engine a level playing field against the Mustang Boss 302-based and Chevy Z-28-based Trans-Am racers.

In the first year of Trans-Am racing with the Javelin, a lot was learned by the men who built and raced the new car. American Motors received excellent exposure, although it cost a small fortune for such a small company to compete against the big boys. The 1968 Trans-Am Javelins did not win any of the 12 races that summer, but did manage to get at least one of the two cars across the finish line during each race. The Javelins were the only factory-backed cars able to make that claim. They finished the 1968 season with six second places in the 12 races and third overall, astounding the auto racing world. Donohue and Penske won the 1968 season for Chevrolet followed by the Bud Moore Mustangs for Ford, the Kaplan Javelins for American Motors, and finally, T/G Racing running Firebirds for Pontiac.

The 1968 cars were sold off to privateers such as Ted Roberts from Southern California, who intended to race the cars independently. Kaplan continued his association with AMC and campaigned the new Javelin. His team prepared the 1969 Trans-Am Javelins at Kaplan's engineering firm and incorporated all that had been learned during the sensational 1968 season. Kaplan and his in-house crew continued to modify and assemble all of their own racing AMC engines. Horsepower was up for the 1969 racing season, but the AMCs weren't the only ones with increases.

In the never-ending search for speed, Kaplan, along with fellow AMC racers Dave Potter and John Martin, had a few special AMC block castings done by a foundry in South Bend, Indiana, at Kaplan's own expense after the close of the 1968 season. With the reworked Traco heads, they had a killer 305 AMC motor. Kaplan said they had to do something because they knew the AMC motor was down 50 horsepower over the top Chevy and Ford motors during the 1968 season, and they knew those boys would find more horsepower for the 1969 season. The two special motors turned 8,000-plus rpm, which gave them a reciprocating mass boost in power over the 1968 engines.

A 305-ci AMC motor was installed in a 1969 Trans-Am Javelin that ran at the first race of the season where it finally had the muscle to stay up with the top Fords and Camaros. It broke near the end of the race, sidelining the car. Martin said AMC Vice President R. W. McNealy was supposed to get the block legalized for homologation by the next race but did not, so the motor was declared illegal. Even with improvements, the Trans-Am Javelins went downhill in 1969 against some fierce competition. The Javelins came in with only 14 points for the 1969 Trans-Am season; the winning Penske Camaros garnered 78 points.

George Follmer gave up his Javelin driver seat due to a commitment to a national tire maker and went back to race for Bud Moore in the Mustangs. Peter Revson bowed out of racing a Javelin because he became a Mercury dealer in late 1968. For 1969, Ford fielded two race teams: the Shelby and Bud Moore.

A little-known fact is that Kaplan was not happy with the trunnion front end of the 1968 and 1969 Javelins because, he said, you could not dial in any antidive under racing conditions. Under hard braking, the Javelin's nose would dive toward the ground, badly upsetting the balance of the car, especially in corners. Increasing roll stiffness to compensate only reduced suspension compliance, a poor trade-off. The 1968-69 (Trans-Am) Mustangs did have antidive characteristics, so AMC copied the front suspension from a light yellow 1968 Mustang they had bought a year before. It was quietly purchased by AMC to see how it stacked up against the 1968 Javelin and

Roy Woods Racing took over for Penske Racing, capturing the SCCA Trans-Am championship title for the second consecutive year in 1972. Most race fans will agree that the Javelin AMX was the meanest-looking Trans-Am race car on the track. Larry Mitchell collection

The 1967 Grant Rambler Rebel SST Funny Car had a fiberglass body on a custom tube-frame chassis. It was powered by an AMC 343 V-8 bored and stroked to 438 cubic inches and running fuel injection and a blower.

With the introduction of the 1967-1/2 343 V-8, four-speed Super-Americans, AMC had done an about-face concerning performance and racing. Rockford Rambler's "Ramblin Red" and others like it appeared at the drag strip and blew the doors off Chevys, Fords, and Plymouths in the same classes.

was hidden at the Burlington, Wisconsin, AMC Proving Grounds close to AMC Engineering in nearby Kenosha.

This new, double balljoint front suspension was made available as a factory option late in the 1969 Javelin production car run at the Kenosha plant. It added over $900 to the cost of a new Javelin, and in 30 years, only one car has ever been documented as a factory-built 1969 Javelin with the 1970 front suspension. The Kenosha-built car was found in 1992 in Melbourne, Australia, by Classic AMX Club International member Ray Sprague.

After the final race of the 1969 race series, AMC made some big changes in the Trans-Am program by firing Kaplan, Jeffords, and the Javelin Racing Team. AMC, speaking collectively, used little diplomacy in treating its racers fair and up front. McNealy, the Harvard grad hired by AMC in the late 1960s and promoted to vice president of marketing services, was deeply involved in controlling AMC's racing activities in

the late 1960s and seemed to be a thorn in many people's sides.

McNealy pulled the rug, cars, and entire Trans-Am racing effort suddenly out from under Kaplan in a hotel room in Riverside, California, in the fall of 1969. He then turned around and announced that AMC had signed Roger Penske Racing Enterprises, together with Mark Donohue driving, to a $1.5 million, three-year Trans-Am contract to build and race the Javelins. Martin said Penske received more money just to relocate than the Kaplan team had been allotted to build and race Javelins throughout the entire 1969 season.

McNealy said, "We selected Roger Penske and Mark Donohue for the Javelin Trans-Am racing program because they have proven their ability to win in the highly competitive, factory-sponsored field." He then said, "With Donohue driving, and preparation of the cars by Penske Racing, we are confident the Javelins will be the team to beat next year."

Penske prepared new 1970 Javelins with Donohue and Peter Revson behind the wheel.

Engine oiling was a problem early in the season and the first four races went to the unbeatable Bud Moore Mustangs. Donohue said in his book, *the unfair advantage*, that AMC was planning to cancel the Penske contract until he finally won a race.

Donohue won his first Trans-Am race in a Javelin at the fifth race of the season at Bridgehampton in the rain and in front of his hometown crowd. Over the course of the season, the problems were worked out and the Javelin was developed. Donohue went on to win 5 of the 11 races in the 1970 Trans-Am series. And Donohue lost the crown by 1 point to Parnelli Jones driving one of the Bud Moore Mustangs. Jones finished the season with 142 points to Donohue's 141. Close, but no cigar.

AMC started to realize the return on its investment in Penske Racing. For the 1971 season, AMC continued its partnership with Roger Penske and Mark Donohue. The team fitted the 1970 Javelins with 1971 sheet metal for the 1971 season series.

The SCCA allowed dry sumps for the first time, and chronic oiling problems with the AMC 305 race engines were finally cured. Jim Travers and Frank Coons of Traco Engineering in California squeezed 450 horsepower out of the AMC 360 motors that were sleeved and stroked to the maximum 305-ci limits. Ten racing motors were prepared for the 1971 races.

Roy Woods Racing (RWR) became the second professional team running Javelins, and Penske sold 6 of the 10 race motors to Woods and also shared technical information. Penske planned to run a single Javelin with Mark Donohue driving and David Hobbs serving as his backup. AMC now had two racing teams, but it proved to be overkill because Ford, Chrysler, and Chevrolet pulled sponsorships, leaving all their race cars without factory backing. For the 1971 Trans-Am season, AMC was the only factory team left and it had two teams with which to earn points.

The Javelins were running the best they ever had, and Donohue's driving was superb. At the opening race of the series on May 8 at Lime Rock, Donohue crossed the finish line an incredible five full laps ahead of the second-place car, a Mustang driven by Tony DeLorenzo. It rained that day and Donohue's skill at driving in the rain on his new Goodyear Blue Streak rain tires played a major role in his win. Two of Roy Woods' Javelins, driven by Peter Revson and Tony Adamowicz, were also in that race.

A Super Stock AMX launches off the line with its wheels in the air on a drag strip years ago. No other AMC car made a bigger impression on skeptics who thought the AMC medium-block 390 wasn't fast when properly modified. The S/S AMX convinced them otherwise. Larry Mitchell collection

The mighty 1969 Hurst-prepared Super Stock AMX drag racer shows its factory hash racing colors. This finely restored example is 100 percent correct as it was delivered to the buyer in 1969. Jerry Heasley

This Super Stock AMC 390 engine is exactly the way it was raced in 1969. This motor propelled the AMX through the quarter-mile in the high 10-second range long before nitrous oxide injection. Jerry Heasley

find no major sponsors at all. Making matters worse, the SCCA wasn't known for large purses at that time. RWR hired George Follmer to drive one car with Roy himself driving the other. Follmer won the opening race by two laps on May 6, 1972, at Lime Rock. At the end of the seven races held that year (three were canceled), RWR (with some points added by Bill Collins) had 48 points, Mustang 34, Firebird 28, and Camaro 24.

AMC had won its second consecutive Trans-Am Championship in 1972. After the 1972 season ended, the Javelins were sold off to Jocko Maggiacomo, who privately raced them in 1973. AMC was out of the picture. The rules had changed for 1973, and the Javelins were now lumped in with Corvettes and Porsches. Attendance had gone down after 1971, and the Trans-Am races would never be the same. Maggiacomo gave it all he had and garnered 1 point for AMC in the 1974 Trans-Am series, 6 in 1975, and 41 in 1976. He won Category I at the eighth race of the season at Pocono. The car and racing parts were eventually sold to the University of Pennsylvania, which played with the car and eventually sold it and all its parts.

The Quest for Quarter-Mile Glory

AMC Performance Activities Director Carl Chakmakian knew AMC had to get credibility by racing cars, especially in drag racing. Young buyers lived and breathed quarter-mile timeslips and bought cars from the companies that had strong racing images. His budget for his efforts was one million dollars, a reasonable amount of cash for the times.

Chakmakian made an agreement with Grant Industries of Los Angeles to make a type of dragster known as a Funny Car. In the early 1960s, these cars were altered-wheelbase cars with the rear axle moved up under the rear windows, leaving a trunk half as long as the whole car. They looked "funny," hence the name.

Grant made piston rings, steering wheels, and the Grant "Flamethrower" ignition systems. He also had a desire for more national publicity. The relationship with American Motors provided increased exposure. Grant Industries President Grant McCoon was asked why he decided to work with AMC on the project. He said, "Rambler is a good automobile, and it's time somebody proved what it can do."

By 1966 these Funny Cars became custom tube frames with fiberglass shell replica bodies that resembled real cars seen on the streets. American carmakers saw advertising opportunities and backed racers to run the cars for points and exhibition. The NHRA (National Hot Rod Association) created special classes at the drags for them to run in, called X/S (Experimental Stock) and Super Experimental Stock.

Grant started with a tube frame, installing an AMC Model 20 rear axle beefed up and with a trick front suspension. A heavily modified Borg-Warner automatic was used, and the motor was the AMC 343 hogged out and stroked to an incredible 438 ci. A GMC 6-71 blower and Enderle fuel injection sat on top. The motor produced 1,200 brake horsepower, spun to 9,000 rpm, and burned a mixture of alcohol and nitromethane. The car initially ran a 4.10:1 rear gear set and tipped the scales at 2,145 pounds.

The fiberglass body was of a 1967 Rebel two-door hardtop stretched 6 inches. Typical of Funny Cars at that time, it had a one-piece body with no opening doors, trunk, or hood. The rear of car was hinged for access to the mechanicals and cockpit. The body was painted Candy Apple Red with a blue stripe dotted with white stars up the center.

The Grant Rambler Rebel and Rebel SST Funny Cars announced to the world that American Motors was now into serious national racing, a complete turnaround from the stand the company announced in 1964 and stuck by until loss of profits put the company on the skids. Grant's driver was "Bonzai" Bill Hayes. The Rebel Funny Car was first run in

Wally Booth teamed up with American Motors to campaign a Pro-Stock Gremlin in the early 1970s. The car attracted a lot of attention for AMC and was competitive at the drags. Larry Mitchell collection

June 1967. During the season, the car raced in 19 cities, set six local track records for its class, and set a national speed record. The car went on display at AMC dealers in the areas it was being raced to produce publicity. A lot of AMC-logo racing freebies were given away and included stickers, hats, jackets, photos, T-shirts, and scale models.

For the 1968 war, a totally new car was built by Grant and AMC. It was driven by Hayden Proffitt and renamed the *Grant Rebel SST*. AMC was eliminating the Rambler name little by little. Proffitt set six local drag strip records that summer. The car consistently ran in the mid-eight-second range at speeds around 180 miles per hour. The 1968 car was painted the new hash red, white, and blue scheme that was now American Motors' racing colors.

At times, drag strip owners would whip up enthusiasm around town by having match races between the various Funny Car makes and sponsors. It was a Chevy-versus-Ford, Dodge-versus-AMC, manufacturer-competition kind of thing the fans crowded the stands for on a summer weekend. When these "unofficial" speed exhibitions were staged, there were no rules. It was simply a show. The GM Funny Cars ran bored and stroked big-block 427s, the Ford racers had a 429 big block, and the Chrysler racers, the world-famous 426

Hemi big block. AMC only had a medium-sized block engine, and this was a handicap that meant the 1968 *Grant Rebel SST Funny Car* could not overcome. The only way the Rebel could win was if its rivals took a dive.

To be more competitive, it was rumored that Grant was allowed to install a Chrysler 426 Hemi for exhibition match racing. Generally, not many people came into the pits in those days, and the body was kept down on the frame to hide the motor.

The Rebel was the only car Grant raced during the 1968 season. Grant and American Motors expanded their Funny Car efforts and created a 1968 Javelin Funny Car named the *Grant Javelin SST Super Funny Car*. The car was made from custom moly tubing with a "flopper" single-piece fiberglass body. The race car used the same 438-ci version of the AMC 343 V-8 that was used in the *Grant Rambler Rebel SST Funny Car*. The car was run at local tracks around the United States, mostly for exhibition. The Javelin Funny Car did not do as well as the Rebel Funny Car, which also received much more publicity.

Grant's Rebel SST Funny Car had been successful in attracting attention to the reborn American Motors Corporation. The progressive AMC dealer network based in Southern California also felt the new Javelin would be a good candidate for a drag racing Funny Car. Doug Thorley was making headers for the Javelin, and a relationship between his company and AMC could produce sales for both. Thorley had won the 1967 NHRA Funny Car

The AMC engine that powered Booth's Pro-Stock Gremlin was a 360 V-8 stroked to 340 ci. It put out 570 horsepower—good enough to put the car into the nines at the strip. Larry Mitchell collection

National Championship with a Chevy-powered Corvair and had a racing reputation going for him.

Thorley had a Funny Car chassis constructed with the engine in the rear, and Berry Plasti Glass produced a 1968 Javelin fiberglass body shell for the car, painted in the hash red, white, and blue pattern that had become the AMC corporate racing paint scheme. The new AMX 390 V-8 was modified to the hilt and a blower was installed. B&M Hydro built a direct-fluid coupler for the car with only an "in and out" shifter. The setup had no driveshaft. In the 1968 season, the car ran a best in the quarter-mile of 8.53 seconds at 182.54 miles per hour.

American Motors felt that drag racing was an important advertising avenue to promote its performance cars. The best car from which to make a factory race car was the AMX, which had far more universal and sporting appeal than the SC/Rambler or the Javelin. George Hurst was on AMC's consulting payroll, and having Hurst Performance make a serious drag car out of the 1969 AMX seemed a logical thing to do. NHRA and AHRA rules required 52 production cars to be modified in order to be classed as super stock drag racers. AMC pulled 53 Frost White 1969 AMXs off the Kenosha assembly line and shipped them to Hurst's Michigan facilities for conversion. The cars' serial numbers appear to have been grouped from A9M397X213560 to A9M397X213613, with dash plaque numbers from 12,567 to 12,620.

The cars were to be known as the S/S AMXs, or Super Stock AMXs. Hurst worked closely with American Motors' Engineering Department to set up the cars to be highly competitive in the NHRA classes SS/D and SS/E. The cars qualified for Formula One C/Stock in AHRA, but most were to compete in the NHRA classes. A majority of the cars were left solid Frost White, although some were painted in the AMC (Trans-Am) racing scheme of red, white, and blue hash. Each vehicle had a charcoal vinyl interior. New owners of the solid white cars could add additional paint colors to their own liking.

The cars were devoid of sound insulation and undercoating, but had to retain stock interiors. No comfort or convenience options were installed to hold total weight to as close to the top of the class weight breaks as possible. A lot of unneeded items such as rocker panel trim, dual horns, front sway bar, and other items were eliminated to shed precious pounds. A large, metal hood scoop was placed on the hood. The S/S AMX tipped the scales at a scant 3,050 pounds.

Suspensions were altered and modified, and forged axles were installed in the AMC Model 20

Pictured is the bizarre Von Piranha AMX. Working with Thoroughbred Motors in Colorado Springs, Colorado, and Bob Bundy AMC in Denver, a man known only as "Von" slit the hood and hung scoops galore on more than 20 1968 AMXs with highly modified 390s. The Von Piranha AMXs, as they were known, were sold as drag and road race cars to buyers.

rear end, along with 4.44:1 gears. Standard AMX torque links were retained for traction control. Cragar SS chrome five-spoke wheels were the wheels of choice.

The 390 motor was removed and reworked, and the heads went to Crane Engineering for heavy modification. The list of high-performance equipment included 12.3:1 Jahns racing pistons, Mallory ignition components, and Doug Thorley headers. A stock cam was installed just to run the motors, and any blueprinting or balancing was up to the new owner before the car went racing. The AMC/Edelbrock cross-ram intake manifold, developed for Trans-Am racing use with two Holley four-barrels, was bolted on. Initially, the motors were rated at only 325 horsepower, but in racing trim, they produced between 405 and 420 horsepower. Later, legal modifications would produce even more horsepower.

Schiefer supplied the high-performance clutch, pressure plate, and special flywheel that were used in the S/S AMXs. The scatter-shield was a solid steel unit from Lakewood, and a removable engine cross-member was made by Hurst to facilitate oil pan removal without pulling the motor. A

Hurst Competition Plus shifter with reverse lock-out was fitted to the Warner Gear T-10 with a 2.23:1 first gear. Ready to run, the car's suggested retail was $5,994 plus tax, title, and destination charges. A warning that the cars were not intended for street use but for "offroad use only" was posted on the window sticker and a special sticker on the door. The fact that buyers had no warranty helped reinforce the disclaimer. AMC wanted as much success as possible for independent owners and was ready, willing, and able to help racers keep the cars in competition.

A lot of original mechanical parts were replaced and modified as problems cropped up. As the bugs were worked out, the S/S AMXs dipped into the low-10-second bracket and records were broken. One of the most notable racers was Shirley Shahan, a pioneer female racer in drag racing. She and her husband, H. L. Shahan, campaigned an S/S AMX for the Southern California American Motors Dealers Association under the name *Drag-On-Lady*. She had driven a Plymouth to a Super Stock Eliminator win in 1966 at the NHRA Winternationals.

Lou Downing was also a big name in racing and drove an S/S AMX called *Pete's Patriot* out of

Land Speed Record Holder Craig Breedlove was hired to build and drive two 1968 AMXs in an attempt to set USAC world speed and endurance records. The new AMX set 106 new records, many of which had been previously set by the Studebaker Avanti.

A rare, private photo of the 1968 Javelin Speed Spectacular Javelins at Bonneville. First from the left is AMC's Performance Activities Director Carl Chakmakian with Craig Breedlove second from the right. The other three men are not identified.

Kearney, Nebraska, for Pete Peterson's AMC dealership. Downing won two class divisional titles in 1969 and 1970, held records, and was Super Stock Eliminator at the NHRA Nationals in 1970. Ed Shaver, a former Arvada, Colorado, resident, ran an S/S AMX owned by John Wolfe Racing and sponsored by toy maker Mattel. The list of S/S AMX owners and their accomplishments with the car is a long one. Numerous records were held by these cars, and Herman Lewis still holds a class record with an S/S AMX today. Not surprisingly, the Hurst S/S AMX ranks as the top collectible production AMX ever made.

Even though Javelins and AMXs grabbed the majority of AMC press at the races, they were not the only AMCs to take to the quarter-mile. Gremlins and Hornets were drag raced from 1972 on. The most famous builders/drivers were Wally Booth, and later Richard Maskin and David Kanners. Booth was AMC-backed until 1974, and his first title win was at the 1974 Gatornationals with his Hornet turning in 8.97 seconds at 152.80 miles per hour. He went on to win the Spring Nationals at Columbus, Ohio, where he ran under the national record. He went on to win the Spring Nationals again in 1976.

Speed Run Cars

Drag racing and Trans-Am road racing were only two elements of AMC's racing program. AMC had its corporate eye on speed run competition as well. Land Speed Record Holder Craig Breedlove of Torrence, California, was put on the payroll at AMC in 1968. He was a hired gun to drive the new 1968-1/2 AMX in speed and endurance runs, and anything else he could come up with to create waves across America to get the press and the American youth interested in the new Javelin. Breedlove and AMC did come up with an additional novel plan.

The idea was to stage an event that might help show how good the new American Motors 290/343 engine was in serious performance other than drag racing—which others were already doing. Breedlove knew the Bonneville Salt Flats very well, having set world land speed records there more than once. His latest record was 600.601 miles per hour in his Spirit of America Land Speed Record car. AMC knew his name would bring a degree of machismo and credibility to his portion of the new AMC racing program.

Breedlove felt that while he was at Bonneville trying to set top speed records with the new AMX, something could be done with Javelins at the same time. Somewhere, the idea of a national contest was hatched. *Car Craft* magazine was the vehicle to get the word out about this contest, where nine winning readers would go to the Bonneville Salt Flats and tune and tinker with three specially prepared 1968 red, white, and blue 343 V-8 Javelins. The object was to pit three, three-person "mechanic" crews against each other in a tuning contest. Each crew would get a Javelin to tune, and then Craig Breedlove would make a top-speed run with the car. The three team members whose Javelin ran the fastest won the three Javelins used in the contest. The fastest Speed Spectacular Javelin ran 161 miles per hour at Bonneville.

Performance Activities Manager Carl Chakmakian hired Breedlove to prepare two AMXs for the USAC (United States Auto Club) speed and endurance record runs at the Goodyear Test Track near San Angelo, Texas, and Bonneville. The cars were modified within USAC rules with chassis help from Kaplan Engineering, and engine work by Traco in California. One car ran in Class C with a modified AMC 290 V-8 and the other ran Class B with a modified AMC 390 V-8. The track was a five-mile banked circle. The object was to run the two cars at over 150 miles per hour and 175 miles per hour, respectively, for certain-hour time periods and a 24-hour total time period. The main drivers were Breedlove and his wife, Lee, with backup driver Ron Dykes.

When the engines were finally shut down, the Breedloves had established 90 new USAC Class C records for the 290 V-8 car averaging 140.790 miles per hour and 16 new records for Class B with the 390 car. At speeds over 175 miles per hour, a dip in the track caused the AMX to become slightly airborne on every lap. The force of the car slamming down on the track caused the Warner Gear T-10 four-speed to fail after eight hours, but it was still, an impressive racing debut for a brandnew automobile that spoke volumes for American Motors' new V-8s.

Breedlove used a blown and injected AMC 390 in one of the two AMX race cars to try to break 200 miles per hour at Bonneville. The weather was bad and Craig found the car was drifting sideways off line as it climbed past 175 miles per hour. He said the calibrated speedometer finally registered over 200 miles per hour, but it was unofficial. Further attempts were not made, as the salt was far too wet to continue.

Breedlove built a small land speed record streamliner for American Motors called the *American Spirit* in 1968. It weighed only 2,000 pounds and was the smallest car of its kind ever constructed. It was to run with three variations of the AMC V-8, all fuel-injected and supercharged in three different classes. Unfortunately, his shop was

AMC's ad agency Wells, Rich and Greene came up with this national ad for car magazines in the spring of 1968. The idea was to show AMC skeptics that the AMX as sports car had the power and the durability to break records—and more than just a few.

flooded and the streamliner was badly damaged. To make matters worse, he had no insurance. Other things went wrong in a short time span and Breedlove suffered bankruptcy, and for a while was completely out of racing. We will never know what might have been because the AMC-powered streamliner never made a run.

AMC in NASCAR Racing

AMC was committed to its road racing, drag racing, speed runs, and stock car racing. In 1969, NASCAR was running a racing series called the NASCAR GT, or Baby Grand National Circuit. AMC decided running a pair of Javelins in this type of oval track racing might help sell the cars in the showrooms, especially in the southern United States.

Two 1969 Javelins were prepared to run in the NASCAR GT factory-backed, but independent of

Jim Paschal raced in NASCAR's Grand American Challenge (a.k.a. Baby Grand National) in a 1970 Javelin. On May 31, 1970, he set a NASCAR Grand American Challenge closed-course speed record at Delaware's Dover Downs. Paschal won 10 victories during the 1970 season and garnered 179 total points against Camaro's 248. Larry Mitchell collection

each other. One car was prepared by Hurst Performance Research for Bob Tullius. Bob Tarozzi, a former engineer for Chrysler's stock car racing program, came to Hurst solely to head the Javelin NASCAR GT program. He handled much of the modification chores.

The other Javelin was race-built by Huggins Tire Sales, Inc., Racing Division of Thomasville, North Carolina. Jim Paschal, a successful NASCAR veteran, was the driver, and Warren Prout did the work on the Huggins Javelin. Prout was a builder for Moore, who raced Cougars and Mustangs in the Trans-Am series. A 343 V-8 was destroked to the 305-ci limit of the engines. The cars sported the American Motors' racing theme of hash red, white, and blue.

It was an impressive first-year effort for AMC. The NASCAR GT Javelins won five of the races in 1969, finished third in the run for manufacturers' championship points, and won the Northern Tour Championship.

Prout and Paschal continued to campaign their cars in NASCAR's Grand American series, formerly called the Grand Touring series. Paschal entered the record books on May 31, 1970 at Dover Downs

International Raceway. He set the world 1-mile closed-circuit speed record for the NASCAR Grand American Challenge series with a lap time of 27.60 seconds at 130.434 miles per hour. During the season, Paschal drove to victory at Bridgehampton, Daytona, Blue Hen, Raleigh, Henry County, and at other venues for a total of 10 victories.

For the 1971 NASCAR GT series, driver Paschal continued to run his 1970 Javelin on the banked oval tracks in the South. Unfortunately, AMC couldn't justify factory support for 1971 and the Javelin was raced privately. Sales of new Javelins and AMC cars in the South simply didn't increase enough to make the effort worthwhile.

AMC and Penske/Donohue entered the 1972 Matador hardtop in NASCAR Winston Cup racing. Due to an inefficient aerodynamic design, the car was not competitive its first year out. The Matador's bright and shining moment came at the 1973 Winston 500 road race held at Riverside, California, where Mark Donohue took the Matador to victory lane. The following year, AMC had reversed its fortunes and produced a car with vastly improved aerodynamics. Stock car racing great Bobby Allison joined the Penske team and guided the Coca Cola–sponsored 1974 Matador coupe to victory at the last race of the season in Ontario, California.

For 1975 the upward trend of success continued. The Matador coupe again won the Riverside 500 at the start of the season as well as the 125-mile qualifying race for the Daytona 500. The other factory drivers and teams were forced to stand up and take notice of the Matador. And, amazingly, the car took second in the Daytona 500 behind winner Benny Parsons driving a Chevy. Other wins came at the Rebel 500 and the Southern 500 run at Darlington. Sadly, the Southern 500 was the last race for the AMC-sponsored Penske Matador. Allison would privately run the car for two seasons a couple of years later, but didn't have much success.

SCCA Road Racing

In 1967, John Martin worked as a mechanic at a Chevrolet dealer in Antioch, Illinois, just down the road from the AMC Kenosha plant. A friend who worked at the plant got him interested in the new 1967 290 and 343 V-8 Americans. Martin bought a new blue two-door sedan and built it into a SCCA A/Sedan racer. Eventually he became an early pioneer in racing AMC products and quietly attained a lot of success.

His American featured a stock 290 V-8 engine, punched out to 305 ci and modified for road racing. Martin set the suspension up under the rules as well as other needed racing alterations. He said the little American was very light compared to his competition and had a higher weight-to-horsepower ratio.

Martin ran SCCA tracks in the Midwest and South against Mustangs, Camaros, Firebirds, and Barracudas. He finished the 1967 season third in national points and was invited to run the national finals at Daytona. At Daytona, Chrysler protested the Rambler, so Martin had to run smaller tube headers for the finals and start at the back of the pack. He had worked his way back up to the front, and nearing the end of the race, when

The 1972 NASCAR racing Matador leads The King himself, Richard Petty, in old number 43 down the front straights. The Matadors were raced in NASCAR for a number of years and won some races, but never the crown. Larry Mitchell collection

This 1970 Javelin SST is the fastest AMC car in history. Equipped with a highly modified, 650-plus-horsepower AMC 390 V-8, it has been clocked on radar at speeds of up to 200 miles per hour on the street. The car has averaged 170 miles per hour for 90 miles of wide-open-throttle legal road racing on a two-lane highway in Nevada in 1997. It is owned and raced by Californians Tony and Rhonda Zamisch. Tony Zamisch

the heat from the motor melted the exhaust valves and the upstart little American was sidelined.

Martin said his American could have won the 1967 SCCA A/Sedan national title if he could have gotten the larger tube headers homologated in time. He also won the famed Milwaukee Mile race and other individual events with the car that summer.

As previously stated, Ronnie Kaplan hired Martin to be crew chief of the new Trans-Am Javelin Team after Martin's success in the 1967 SCCA racing season. As crew chief, Martin was able to apply his knowledge of mechanics and experience of racing the American. He engineered the chassis, suspension, and engines in 1968 and 1969 for the Javelins. Martin said, "My goal was to be a driver on the team when a vacant seat came up and that was the agreement I made with Ronnie Kaplan when I joined the team." Eventually, he got a ride.

While he served as crew chief for the Kaplan Javelin Trans-Am team, he continued to race the American in A/Sedan. Martin finished second in national points in 1968 driving the American. At the last event of the year at Riverside, AMC asked him to switch from his American to a Kaplan-prepared Javelin.

For the following competition season, Racing, Inc., a small group of AMC employees, fielded an AMX in the SCCA B/Production class. They worked at the AMC headquarters in Detroit in the Styling and Engineering departments. Racing, Inc, took a 1969 343 V-8, four-speed AMX and modified it to fit the rules of the B/Production class. Ike Knupp, supervisor for the electrical lab at AMC, was the sole driver.

After the 10 divisional races for the summer, Knupp's red, white, and blue AMX had five first-place finishes, two second places, and one third, enough to win the Midwest Divisional title in B/Production. Their closest competitor was a Corvette that had a record of winning in recent years and was second in overall points going to the finals.

The team went to the national championship final held at the Daytona International Speedway on November 30, 1969. The AMX was ahead of a Corvette in the final few laps when the T-10 four-speed locked up in second gear. Ike had to maintain a steady speed in second so as to not over-rev the motor. The Corvette passed the AMX down the front straight and crossed the finish line, stealing the win. The AMX finished only a few seconds behind. It was a disappointing end to a Cinderella year, but an incredible show of serious performance for American Motors' AMX.

From 1971 to 1981, Team Highball, an IMSA-oriented racing team out of North Carolina, raced showroom stock Gremlins, Hornets, and Pacers with AMC backing. True gutted and modified race cars, they were powered by highly modified 232 six-cylinder engines with over 250 brake horsepower. The cars ran for nearly 10 years and captured the IMSA manufacturers titles in 1975 and 1976.

The Silver State Open Road Race Challenge

Some of the most amazing demonstrations of AMC performance has happened in the last 15 years. A handful of AMC owners and drivers have competed in and set records in a flat-out, wide-open-throttle road race down a stretch of two-lane highway in Nevada. It is the Silver State Open Road Race Challenge sanctioned by the American Indy Car Series.

Tony Zamisch and his wife Rhonda from California own a modified production 1970 390 Mark Donohue Javelin. They are the fastest man and woman to officially drive a production-based American Motors car at any time in history. Tony has been clocked on Nevada's Highway 318 at 192 miles per hour, and his wife has attained over 180 miles per hour. They both averaged over 160 miles per hour for the first 90 miles. Others who have joined the "AMC Century and a Half on the Street Club" (over 150 miles per hour top Speed) competing in the Silver State Race are Larry Mitchell in his red 1969 AMX. Roger Scott of Colorado broke the 125 mile per hour top speed barrier in his 1976 232-ci inline six SCCA-legal Pacer coupe. Lamar Petersen of Iowa accomplished the same feat in his ex-Los Angeles Police Department 1973 Matador. These cars have proven beyond a doubt, that AMC performances are still a force to be reckoned with in the modern days of overhead cam and four-valves-per-cylinder engines.

John Martin of Antioch, Illinois, was a pioneer in AMC racing with his new 1967-1/2 343 V-8 Super-American. He won the Midwest Divisional Title and was second at the national finals in SCCA A/Sedan racing for the 1967 season.

The lone surviving 1969 Pikes Peak Hillclimb Pace/Courtesy AMX that Bobby Unser drove during race week in 1969. The reproduction decals are correct for June 29, 1969. The skyline of Denver, Colorado, is in the background. Bruce Jacobsen

The only AMX to have officially raced in the history of the Pikes Peak Hillclimb is this 1969 model, which was owned, prepared, and raced by this author in Vintage Division, 1987. Dave McHattie

Pikes Peak Hillclimb

After AMC pulled its factory support from racing by mid-1975, a number of dedicated AMC racers continued to race the cars. A handful of AMC drivers have raced AMC cars in the world famous Pikes Peak Hillclimb in Colorado Springs, Colorado. Jim Happ, former mechanic for Randall AMC in Mesa, Arizona, drove 360 V-8 Gremlins and Spirits in numerous hillclimbs over the years. Professional racer Roger Mears piloted a 360 V-8 in a 1979 Spirit AMX in 1979. Ex–Trans-Am privateer Ted Roberts of Yucca Valley, California, ran a genuine 1969 Kaplan-prepared Trans-Am Javelin in 1986 and 1987. And Larry Mitchell of Arvada, Colorado, ran a 1969 390 AMX in 1987. Off-road Legend Don Adams of Buena Vista, Colorado, has raced AMC 401-powered Jeeps over the years and has won class titles and set records in the Pikes Peak Hillclimb as well.

AMC Goes Off Road

Yes, AMC even ventured off-road during the musclecar era. Actor James Garner ran a team of highly modified two- and four-wheel-drive 1969-1/2 390 SC/Ramblers in the 1969 Baja 500, where they finished one, two, and three in Sedan class and won Class I, all with basically stock engines—impressive performances for using the Rambler SC/Rambler like a Jeep.

Epilogue

American Motors, born in 1954, proudly carried on the Rambler name that had dated back to the beginning of the twentieth century. The name became an albatross by the mid-1960s and had to be replaced by AMC in order to survive. Compared to the Big Three, American Motors made only a handful of serious performance cars in an eight-year period. The cars lacked the legendary stature of the big-block cars from Ford, General Motors, and Chrysler, but they held their own on the streets and race tracks when classed with their Big Three equals and are still setting some records today. From the cute 1968 AMX to the wild 1969 SC/Rambler, they are collected and loved in modern times by people around the world who want something different and unique.

In 1987, Chrysler, in a surprise move, bought all the stock from AMC's partner Renault and enough from the Stock Exchange to gain control of AMC. Chrysler took over AMC in order to grab the Jeep Division. Chrysler stopped AMC car production and discarded millions of dollars of AMC parts, taking a tax write-off. Chrysler literally bulldozed company buildings and threw away precious history. The AMC hobbyists are the losers. For these reasons, most true AMC collectors wish to remain pure AMC and feel American Motors died in 1987—it does not live on in Chrysler.

The vintage 1969 AMX 390 racer, built and driven by Jim Weyand of Littleton, Colorado, is captured on Lookout Mountain, above Golden, Colorado. The AMX, AMC's bold statement in high-performance, didn't come close to capturing the marketshare of the Mustang or the Camaro, but on the street the blindingly fast two-seater kept up with its contemporary competition.